The Complete Guide to
Functional Writing in English

The Complete Guide to
FUNCTIONAL WRITING IN ENGLISH

M SARADA

A Sterling Paperback

STERLING PAPERBACKS
An imprint of
Sterling Publishers (P) Ltd.
A-59, Okhla Industrial Area, Phase-II,
New Delhi-110020.
Tel: 26387070, 26386209; Fax: 91-11-26383788
E-mail: mail@sterlingpublishers.com
www.sterlingpublishers.com

The Complete Guide to
Functional Writing in English
© 2006, Sterling Publishers (P) Ltd.
ISBN 978 81 207 2923 0
Reprint 2007, 2008, 2011

All rights are reserved.
No part of this publication may be reproduced, stored in a retrieval system or transmitted, in any form or by any means, mechanical, photocopying, recording or otherwise, without prior written permission of the original publisher.

Printed in India
Printed and Published by Sterling Publishers Pvt. Ltd., New Delhi-110 020.

Preface

The purpose of the book, *Functional Writing in English* is to help the advanced learners to fulfil certain social, business and academic functions encountered by them in day-to-day life. It is meant for the learners who have taken a degree or studied English for 10 or 12 years and have the habit of reading newspapers and magazines or journals. It aims to teach the skills of writing for particular functions like describing people to introduce, give an eyewitness account, an obituary note etc., or to give a long account of someone such as a profile, tribute and short-biography.

The book also intends to help the learners who are ready to enter the job market or have just got one. Generally, any job entails the workforce to do multiple activities and one among them is to communicate with their peers, superiors, and other institutes, customers and the public at large, about the work done by them or going to take up, through writing. One such important duty is to write proposals when they take up a project and prepare reports after they finish it. Writing a report is a necessary part of their work as it reveals to their boss or the people concerned about the work done by them. And reports serve as a record also. Some staff may need to give presentations, prepare papers when they go to a seminar or executive meetings, or publish papers in their company magazines. So a smart employee needs to update her/his writing skills constantly. No way. By using the language for various purposes effectively, s/he becomes skilled in the craft of writing and better qualified than others for a suitable job or promotion.

But all may not go for work soon after their graduation or postgraduation but take up research. On the academic front, the book aims to help the learners who pursue higher studies, like postgraduation or research. And higher education involves the learners to practise reference skills and advanced writing skills. Hence the book includes a module on scholarly writing also.

The book tries to be different from the run-of-the-mill kind, by giving 'hands on experience'. The exercises help the learners to have a real life like situation and get intense practise in using the language to suit their needs. With this aim, the book is divided into four modules—

I Describing People
A. Introducing, B. Eyewitness Accounts, C. Missing, D. Obituary
E. Account of People— 1. Profile 2. Tribute 3. Short-biography.

II Proposals
A. Technical, B. Non-technical

III Reports
A. Newspaper Reports, B. Reports based on Interviews
C. Business Reports, D. Reports of Experiments
E. Reporting of Meetings (Minutes)

IV Thesis Writing
A. Dissertation, B. Term Papers, C. Research Paper(s), D. Doctoral Thesis

As a part of the interactive approach, pair work and group work exercises are given with a view to cultivate 'reader awareness' and promote discussion among the learners. Every writing task is followed by a model exercise and other exercises are to be done by the learners at the end of the module.

Contents

I Describing People — 1
- Introducing
- Eyewitness Accounts
- Missing
- Obituary
- Accounts of People

II Writing a Proposal — 28
- Technical
- Non-technical

III Writing Reports — 42
- Newspaper Reports
- Reports Based on Interviews
- Business Reports
- Reports of Experiments
- Reporting of Meetings (Minutes)

IV Scholarly Writing — 81
- Dissertation
- Term Papers
- Research Paper
- Doctoral Thesis

Glossary — 111
Biblography — 112

I

Describing People

Writing is a way of learning and a continuous process in a civilised person's life. It is not only a product of thinking but thinking itself. It is a kind of output which results from voracious reading and long experience or maturity. May be for that reason, writing comes to the last in the four major skills of the language – listening, speaking, reading and writing. Sometimes a writer does not know her/his ideas or views until s/he puts them down. S/he has to find out first precisely what they have to say and that is possible only by writing. Writing is a tool like a diagram, map or graphics to express oneself, her/his views, ideas or to give information. It provides training in organising ideas and helps one to cultivate a style of their own finally. The rich rewards of writing are self-satisfaction and confidence. As you progress in your studies from one level (standard) to another, your needs of writing varies. In the same way, your needs grow after entering a career and are varied from time to time. Hence, writing is an on going process and one has to trim her/his oars till they reach perfection in the skill.

In this book, you learn advanced writing skills for social, career and academic purposes. What follows is a set of functional writing tasks which are necessary for various social purposes like describing people to give an account of someone, for business purposes like writing a proposal or a report and academic purposes like writing a dissertation, term papers or thesis etc. Thus, by using the language for various purposes effectively, s/he becomes skilled in the craft of writing and better qualified than others for a suitable job, promotion or pursuing higher studies.

You come across various situations in day-to-day social life wherein you need to describe people for various purposes. Sometimes you have to *introduce* someone to another through a letter by describing the person, or give an account about someone as an eyewitness about a robber or a person involved in a road accident, to an official to *identify* the person, or give a short account of a dead person, in an *obituary* note in a newspaper or a journal. Or you give a note – *Wanted* to a newspaper to *trace* someone who ran away from home or a note about a criminal who escaped from a jail. Besides, you may write a brief sketch of a celebrity giving an account of life, her/his achievements and rewards, by way of a *tribute* or simply *the profile* of a person. In all these writing tasks whether short or long what you do mainly is *describing people* for various purposes like introducing, identifying/recognising, tracing and giving a profile etc., using the narrative technique. What are these various purposes?

Various purposes—
- To introduce someone
- To identify/recognise someone
- To trace someone who left home or any place
- To give an eyewitness account
- To write an obituary account of someone to a newspaper/journal
- To pay a tribute in writing, give a profile or sketch
- To describe the life and achievements of someone in the form of a short-biography

Read the following text

> Yogamaya was about forty. The years had added dignity but no flabbiness to her limbs. Fair skinned, her complexion was radiant, the hair cropped close as is the custom with Hindu widows, her eyes filled with the peace of motherly devotion, her smile gentle and calm, her figure draped in coarse white cotton, the head covered. Her immaculate, beautiful feet were bare. As Amit touched them in respectful greeting, he felt the benediction of a goddess thrill through his veins.

[From: Rabindranath Tagore's *Farewell My Friend,* Pub : 1956; Mumbai : Jaico Pub. House, 1983. (P 25)]

Discussion

In the above text, the writer describes the lady character, Yogamaya, to introduce her to the readers in the novel. He gives a note of her physical appearance so minutely as if you see her before you. He gives the details of her age, complexion, hairstyle, dress, feet, and smile etc. He gives a few details of her personality too that she is gentle, calm and motherly devotion personified etc.

When you describe someone for a particular purpose, what do you include in the description?

What to describe?

- **Physical Appearance** (description) or how does s/he look like?
  1. Height and weight, 2. Complexion, 3. Colour of the eyes, 4. Hair colour and hairstyle, 5. Dress, 6. Moustache, or beard style, 7. Personality

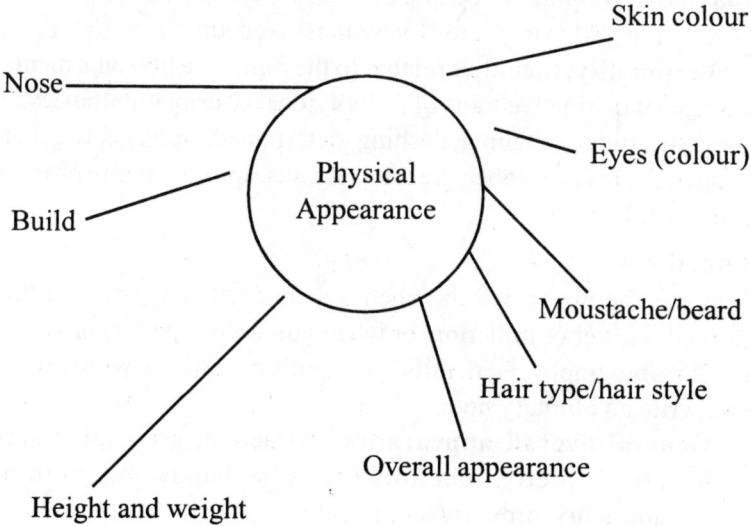

Before going into the details of how to describe people, you need to be familiar with certain vocabulary necessary and distinguish the words connected with physical appearance and personality. The following words will help you—

Face: Oval, round, skinny, bony, pretty
Nose: flat, snub, sharp
Height: very tall, of medium height, short, a good build
Weight: very fat, lean, very lean, lanky, sturdy
Complexion: fair, dark, brown, sallow, medium
Colour of the eyes: blue, black, brown, green, hazel eyes
Hair colour: black, brown or copper colour or red, blond, auburn
Hair type: straight, curly, wavy, soft, long or short, cut hair, bobbed hair etc.

Functions
The details of physical appearance like height, weight, complexion, eyes and hairstyle are necessary when you *identify, recognise, introduce or trace* a person. These functions may be done either through a letter, fiction, and newspapers or any journals through the written mode or orally when you speak to somebody. Generally, you find description of people in newspapers in notifications like 'Wanted 'or 'Missing' and 'Eyewitness Accounts'.

Personality: (qualities related to the mind or a person's mental makeup or distinctive traits of an individual) Curious, enthusiastic, energetic, quiet, outgoing, dashing, determined, fiery, gentle, short tempered, pleasant, sober, graceful, serious, spirited (high-spirited), self-confident etc.

Functions
You use the above words when you introduce a person either through a letter or in fiction, or when you write a profile or sketch or short-biography. Generally, you don't need these words when you write an obituary note.

- **General overall appearance:** attractive, graceful, smart, beautiful, pretty, nice-looking, very handsome, nothing extraordinary, ordinary looking etc.

Functions
You may use the above words while writing a profile/tribute/short-biography or introducing a character in fiction,
- **Short account of life, education and career:**

Describing People **5**

1. Where one is born and brought up, 2. Details of education, 3. Career, 4. Personality
5. Achievements and awards, 6. Field of interest, (s) 7. Personal goals etc.

Functions

You may give some or all the above details when you write a tribute, profile or short-biography of some individual. For obituary you give the achievements and the contribution of the person in his/her field with a short account of the life of the deceased person in the case of a celebrity.

Note

The number of details and length of the note depends on the purpose for which you are describing someone. Better you keep in mind always the target reader and the purpose for which you are writing the note.

Example

Read the following text

> In the half-hour that Mother Teresa sat in the Lieutenant Governor's chamber, I was able to observe her closely. Her face was deeply lined, even a little shrunken. Yet her diminutive* frame only enhanced her obvious magnetism. Her brown eyes twinkled constantly. She appeared to be perceptive and remarkably practical. She could hardly be oblivious of the emotion she aroused in others but she herself was cheerfully unsentimental. Her vocabulary was limited. She also said 'Thank God' a lot, not in any especially religious sense but as a kind of punctuation mark: 'It's hot day, thank God', and I' am glad I came, thank God'. I observed that she wore her sari with grace, something few European women are able to do. ─────────────────────────. It was her hands and her feet, however that betrayed her arduous life. Her fingers were gnarled and twisted and her feet, encased in rough, ungainly sandals, were misshapen. ─────────────────────────P. 13:
> Sister Breen said, 'Mother Teresa, 'was always very simple and very nice. There was nothing extraordinary about her. Just that she was a very simple, ordinary girl. Very gentle, full of fun. Enjoyed everything that went on.

[From: *Mother Teresa,* Navin Chawla, Pub: 1993; Penguin Books India, 2002. P xiii & 13]

───────────

* Remarkably small

Discussion

The above text gives a descriptive account of Mother Teresa giving details of her physical appearance and a short-note about her personality.

Words like — 'face deeply lined, even a little shrunken, a diminutive frame, brown eyes, wore a sari gracefully, hands and her feet —betrayed arduous life, fingers gnarled and twisted and her feet encased in rough ungainly sands, were misshapen—— give details of *physical appearance* such as — her face, eyes, hands, fingers, feet, height, dress and footwear etc. And the other set of words like— perceptive, remarkably practical, cheerful, unsentimental, graceful, very simple, ordinary girl, nothing extraordinary, gentle, full of fun etc. —— give certain details about her *personality* that she is a simple ordinary looking person. The writer through the above description gives a pen picture of Mother Teresa.

In the above text, the writer's purpose is to *introduce* Mother Teresa to his readers in the beginning itself.

You describe someone close to you when you introduce him/her to another. You give the details of physical appearance, field of interest, hobbies, and career goals. Sometimes you have to introduce yourself giving an account of yourself when you have to meet someone for the first time in a party or be a guest to someone who has never seen you before or sometimes in an interview.

1.1 Introducing someone

When you introduce someone in your family to a friend or a colleague what details do you give for the purpose of introducing?

Example

My sister is doing her Masters in Business Administration, and is in the last semester, at Miranda College, Delhi. She is two years younger to me but taller than me, 5ft. 5, does not have anything in common with me in looks, habits or nature. She resembles more my mother. Unlike my mother she often wears jeans and tops or *Churidar*. Her brown eyes, flat nose, fair complexion, thick curly hair reminds my mother of her age. She loves classical music and watches old Hindi movies. After her MBA she wants to take GMAT exam and join my elder brother's company in Florida, US.

Discussion
When you introduce someone in your family to someone close to you, give the particulars of physical appearance, habits and interest and their career and goals in life. But when the person whom you introduce is before you then don't give details of physical appearance but his/her field of interests, present career and future plans of career etc, in the beginning. And later, the two persons will talk to themselves and know more about each other. The few details you give should help the two to start a dialogue and know each other.

1. 2 Eyewitness Accounts

Example 1
It is what Mr Aloknath reported to the circle inspector of Delhi, Chandni Chowk, about a robbery he witnessed at the tea-stall.

Read the following text
As far as I remember, on that day, Feb 18th, around 4 o' clock, I was getting down from my car with my 4-year-old son to go to the 'Food world' which was on the opposite side of the road. When I was crossing the road to go to the shop, there was a tea-stall near the entrance of the shop. I found before the tea-stall, a farmer standing with the turban on his head, thick-glass spectacles, with white dhoti, and half-sleeved blue shirt, holding a purse in his hand. He must be above 60 in age or so, very dark in complexion, and very lean bent with hunchback. Just when he was opening his purse, with a bundle of currency notes, and ready to pay to the tea-stall keeper, two young sturdy men got down from a Royal Enfield bike. They must be aged above 30 and both were very dark, rough looking and were sweating badly. One of them was tonsured and clean shaved and wore black colour spectacles and a snuff coloured, striped shirt stood by the side of their bike. The other person, with black unshaved beard, uncombed curly hair and dressed in blue shorts and yellow full-sleeved shirt, rushed violently towards the

farmer, folding his sleeves up, threatened the latter with his eight inches sharp knife and snatched the purse from the hands of the farmer. The farmer fell down screaming loudly. Before the neighbouring vendors went to the rescue of the farmer, the duo fled on their motorbike.

Example 2
Here is another example wherein you find the account given by the eyewitness about the **road accident** *and the people involved with it.*

A security guard, at *Ganapati Function Hall,* witnessed a road accident wherein Kiran Karthik was killed by a speeding lorry. He reported the incident to the RTO (Road Transport Officer) when the latter asked him to give an account of what he witnessed ——

Read the following text:
What I remember is this— a motorcycle borne young man aged 20 or 25, wearing helmet, white shorts and white high collar t-shirt, was riding at a slow pace, along the extreme left of the road at Kachiguda (an area in Hyderabad). It seems he was on his way to Municipal Corporation of Hyderabad (MCH) playground around 7.00 a.m. on Feb 18, 2004, for a cricket practise session, as the things with him indicated.

Around that time, just before our second gate, when I was outside the gate, just ready to hand over the charge to another guard, a speeding lorry rammed into the motorbike from behind, knocking the young man over. Soon, the young fellow fell flat and the bike also fell on him and his helmet thrown off. A passerby shifted Kiran who was bleeding profusely to the Durgabai Deshmukh Hospital where he succumbed to the injuries.

Later, the traffic police found from the license papers of the victim that he was L Kiran Karthik, a resident of Tilaknagar and second year B Com student of Arora College, Hyderabad.

Discussion
From the above two accounts, it is clear that the accounts given by the eyewitnesses should include details like time, date and place of the incident happened and particulars of the people involved

like age, height, complexion, dress etc. Unlike in a robbery or theft case, one should give particulars of speed, directions of the vehicle and how one is going, on the left or right side of the road etc., with regard to any road accident.

Note
1. Generally, these incidents such as robbery or road accidents, must have happened at least some hours before one reports it to the official concerned. So the reporter should use *past tense* and *reported speech* while giving the description of the people involved in it.
2. In the case of Eyewitness Accounts of any kind one need not give the details regarding personality of the people but more details of physical appearance are needed for the purpose of identifying the people involved in the accident.

1. 3 Missing

Missing:

Read the text in the box and the description of a person 'Missing'.

[From: *The Hindu*, March 23, 2004]

Discussion

While reading the above account, you might have noticed that the essential details of the physical appearance of the missing person are given to recognise or identify him. Age, height, complexion and the photo are given. Most important is the contact number which is given so that if the person is found, the information can be passed on. The details or particulars are such that any person can easily recognise the missing person. So it is better to give as many details as possible to supplement the details shown in the photo.

1.4 Obituary

In fact, *obituary* is a register of deaths or a notice or announcement of someone's death in the newspaper. Generally, you find two kinds of obituary. One is that you find usually in newspapers which is published on payment. This kind of obituary is inserted by the members of the family of the deceased to give an intimation of the person's death and the date of last rites. But this section does not deal with it for study.

Another kind of obituary, which you are going to study, is that which is published by newspapers as a part of news when a celebrity or a person of repute dies. This account includes a short biographical note, the achievements and contribution of the deceased, along with the date of death and other particulars. Sometimes it includes condolences sent by important people. There is no hard and fast rule for the length of the obituary. Generally, if the deceased person is of high profile, the account will be lengthy.

Example 1

Read the following

Science Writer dead

By our Special Correspondent

NEW DELHI, April 3. Noted science writer Dilip M. Salwi died here on Friday following a heart attack. He was 52.

He is survived by his wife and two children.

    A post-graduate in astrophysics from the Delhi University, Mr. Salwi has authored more than 50 books, many of them bestsellers.

He made it to the Limca Book of Records for two consecutive years – 1998 and 1999.

On the first occasion, his name was included for his science fiction, "Fire on the Moon," which sold more than three lakh copies.

The second time, it was for writing the largest number of popular science books for children.

Mr. Salwi is a recipient of several awards, including the children's Book trust award for scientists of India, and the Department of Science and Technology's NCSTC National Prize for popularisation of science among children.

[The Hindu, April 4, 2004]

Example 2

Read the following:

Obituary

M.S. SUBBULAKSHMI
1916 — 2004
ODE TO A NIGHTINGALE

The singing legend lives on in her *suprabhathams* and *bhajans*

When Jawaharlal Nehru heard Carnatic vocalist M. S. Subbulakshmi sing, he said, "What am I, a mere prime minister before the Queen of Music." The voice that moved the world will be heard no more.

An artist extraordinaire, Subbulakshmi had the unique ability to transform the singing experience from the mundane to the divine. A rich, resonant timbre, complete *shruti* arrangement, correct diction and the raga *bhava*—it was a rare combination that created the legend. Unlike today's musicians trapped in external fineries, Subbalakshmi had an instinctive feel for the meaning of the text and each word she so aptly selected stood out like a gem.

Subbulakshmi, or Kunjamma as she was fondly called, was the daughter of Madurai Shanmukhavadivu, a *veena* player. With a violinist for sister, a brother who played the *mridangam* and the mellifluous environs of Madurai, singing came more naturally to her than talking. So Subbulakshmi's first performance came at the age of 10 and thereafter music became the habit of a lifetime, as did awards and adulation. After her marriage in 1940, her husband and freedom fighter, T. Sadasivam, took charge of her career. In fact, when she was conferred the Bharat Ratna in 1998, she said, "On this occasion I cannot but think of the loving care and guidance I received from my late husband all through my life."

In a way and despite her husband's support, Subbulakshmi was a feminist. Having breached the bastion of male singers, she was happy to see an increasing number of women enrolling in music colleges and participating in temple festivals. In 1968, when the Music Academy honoured her with the Sangeetha Kalanidhi, she said, "In conferring the honour, the academy has sought to honour the womanhood of this country."

While sitar maestro Pandit Ravi Shankar popularised Hindustani Classical music abroad, Subbulakshmi introduced Carnatic music to the West. Her biggest contribution to Carnatic music was the revival of the *kritis* of the 15th century composer Annamacharya. Subbulakshmi also acted in four films: *Sevasadanam, Sakuntalai, Savitri* and *Meera.*

After *Meera,* Mahatma Gandhi picked her to sing two of his favourite bhajans, *Vaishnav janto* and *Hari tum haro jan ki bhir.* It was also after M*eera* that she decided to dedicate herself to classical and devotional music. A musician who bridged the regional gap, Subbulakshmi sang in 10 languages, be it the Marathi *abhang,* the Hindi bhajan, the verses of Guru Nanak or Rabindra Sangeet.

Subbulakshmi was indeed an icon who could bring the world to its knees: her renderings moved violinist Yehudi Menuhin to tears, Bade Ghulam Ali Khan called her Suswarlakshmi Subbulakshmi, while Helen Keller once said, " You sing like an angel." She could captivate the people with an occasional lift of an eyebrow and a beatific smile—meant not for the audience but for the divine. "Indian music is oriented solely to the end of divine communication. If I have done something in this respect, it is entirely due to the grace of the Almighty who has chosen my humble self as a tool," she said.

Subbulakshmi is not dead. She is alive in the temples, the *suprabhathams,* the *kritis* and the bhajans. She will remain in that divine voice forever.

[By S. Sahaya Ranjit, 'Ode to a Nightingale' from *India Today,* Dec 27, 2004]

Discussion

The above two obituary notifications are different from each other in certain ways. The first one on Dilip M Salwi, a great scientist is a short one and begins with a note of his death, cause of death and the age at the time of his death. Later the note includes the scientist's contribution as a popular science writer and his awards.

The second obituary on M S Subbulakshmi's is a longer one than the first one because the latter is a celebrity. Besides, this note does not give any particulars of death like date and cause of death.

It just gives the period of her life: 1916 –2004. Later the note deals with M S Subbulakshmi's unique quality of singing, her early life, singing career, a few movies she acted and her awards and titles.

Note
While writing an obituary note, there is no need of giving particulars of physical appearance which is necessary in the case of eyewitness account and wanted/missing notification.

Generally, the reporter or a special correspondent of the newspaper prepares an obituary when a celebrity or an important person dies. The length of the note depends on the importance of the person died. Some of the obituaries may contain condolence messages too sent by important persons like president or prime minister.

1. 5 Accounts of People
A. Profile B. Tribute C. Short-biography
You have come a long way from introducing someone or introducing yourself, eyewitness account (report), wanted/missing and obituary note' (account) to profile/sketch and short-biography. In all these modules you have learnt the skill of describing people. In the case of, 'eyewitness accounts,' 'obituary' or 'wanted' and others, the main focus is on physical appearance like height, weight, hair style, dress etc., but in the next module which you are going to be introduced i.e., profile/tribute short-biography you learn and practise other aspects of describing people like personality, education, professional or personal profile, contribution and achievements of a person along with some general aspects or events of one's life.

In your social life, you come across various incidents, occasions or a ceremony wherein you pay encomiums (praise) or write a tribute/brief sketch/profile of a person. The incident may be someone getting an award, honour, birth centenary or sad occasions like someone's death.

A. Profile

Example

Read the following profile

Satyajit Ray

One may not find a film fan who does not know the name of Satyajit Ray, the renowned film director. Ray's name is synonymous with his famous film *Pather Panchali*. He was India's first filmmaker who received international acclaim from Euro-American Festival and Art House. He produced films based on ideology, contemporary issues and conflicts. Besides being a film director, he was also a producer, noted writer of short stories and detective fiction.

Born in Kolkata on May 2, 1921, Satyajit Ray lost his father, Sukumar Ray, when he was just two and a half years old. But he was lucky enough to live in a joint family with loving uncles and aunts at Gorpar, southern Kolkata. He looked very smart with big eyes and clad in cotton dhoti. Theirs was an intellectual and affluent family and many of them are great artists and writers today. In 1880s the family embraced 'Brahmo Samaj', a reaction against Christianity but a sect within Hindu society. The progressive outlook and rational thinking of the Samaj strongly influenced Ray and it was reflected in his movies.

At school, though lagged behind in sports, Satyajit excelled in art. He became a film fan and regularly started reading Hollywood magazines and listening to Western classical music. He would pick up gramophone records at flea markets. He matriculated when he was just fifteen. After graduating from the Presidency College, he stayed for a while at Tagore's Kalabhavan, Shantiniketan (1940-42) and practised painting under Nandalal Bose. He started his career as a commercial artist.

Ray was a versatile genius who carved a niche for himself in the film world. When he was very young he founded the *Calcutta Film Society* in 1947 with Chidananda Das Gupta et al which introduced him to European and Soviet cine world. His first film, *Pather Panchali* received many accolades both at home and abroad. Rabindranath Tagore was Ray's artistic and intellectual mentor.

Ray made some of Tagore's stories like *Teen Kanya*, *Charulata*, and *Ghare Bhaire* into films which became very popular all over the country. His films reflected the realistic themes of the late 19th century. The films produced in 1960s depicted the conflict between urban culture and rural oppression and those of 1970s showed a major shift and focused on the contemporary Kolkata. Apart from feature films, he made his foray into documentary films and movies for children.

Satyajit Ray's range and versatility can be gauged by his contribution in other fields too. He was an editor of a children's magazine, *Sandesh* founded by his grandfather, Upendra Kishore Ray. He published numerous short stories some of which were filmed by his son Sandeep Ray in two TV serials called *Satyajit Ray Presents*. He was also a producer, screenwriter and graphic designer. He also provided music for *Shakespeare Walla* (1965).

The numerous National and foreign awards bestowed upon him are an evidence of his great contribution to the film world. Some of them are – Padmashree – 1958; Padmabibhushan –1965; Magasaysay Award – 1967; Sangeet Natak Academy –1986.

Further, he received foreign awards like— Special Moscow Film Festival Award, 1979; Cannes Film Festival Award, 1982; Fellowship of The British Film Institute in 1983 and many universities at home and abroad honoured him with Doctor of Letters. In addition, France awarded him the most prestigious Le´gion d'Honneur in 1987. Finally in 1992, he received an Oscar from Hollywood for Lifetime Achievement in filmmaking. The same year our country bestowed on him 'Bharat Ratna', the highest civilian award.

[Adapted from: Aditi De's *'Lights! Camera! Action!*, *The Hindu*, March 13, 2004 and *Encyclopaedia of Indian Cinema*, New Rev. Edition, New Delhi; OUP, 1999]

Discussion

Profile or sketch is a brief account of a person. This brief account includes both personal and professional profile but does not include praise, usually. It narrates factual accounts of one's life, education, career, achievements, and contribution in the chosen field or specialised field of the person about whom you write briefly. Sometimes you may find critical evaluation of his career or life unlike in the tribute'.

In the above profile, on Satyajit Ray, it begins with a brief introduction about the field of Satyajit Ray who is remembered as a great filmmaker. Later the second and third paragraphs deal with a short account of the life and education and favourable circumstances in which Ray developed his interest in filmmaking, respectively. Another short paragraph deals with his professional career till he became a celebrity. Next, the writer deals with Ray's other contributions related to filmmaking. Finally, the writer list briefly the prestigious awards and honours of Ray.

In the above text, a very brief account of Satyajit Ray's life was given, as it is a profile, only.

B. Tribute

Example

Read the following text

Justice V M Tarkunde who died on March 22, 2004, was one of the increasingly rare breed of judges of the past who had interests in public affairs outside the field of law. From his early days in 1936 he was a follower of M N Roy and joined his Radical Democratic Party. After its dissolution he was active in Radical Humanistic Movement, which replaced the Radical Democratic Party and was the editor of the *Radical Humanist* for many years. After his resignation as a judge of the Bombay High Court in 1969 he was active in movements to secure civil liberties. In 1974 with Jayaprakash Narayan he founded Citizens for Democracy. He was also one of the founders of the Peoples Union for Civil Liberties in 1976. Until his death at the age of 94 he was the cause of civil liberties and wrote frequently on these subjects.

Tarkunde was a liberal intellectual who appeared to have strayed into the legal profession. His conspicuous character as a judge was his overwhelming desire to arrive at what he conceived to be a just decision in the case before him even if it is meant bending the facts and the law for that result. He apparently believed in Bassanio's plea to Portia in *Merchant of Venice*: "Wrest once the law to your authority; to do a great right do a little wrong".

Tarkunde was a judge from 1957 to 1968. In those days judges did not had the expansive and liberal scope of their judicial power, which they have today. Tarkunde's decisions therefore appeared to be made to suit his notions of equity. I remember typically two cases decided by him. In Sophie Kelly's case, he set aside the government's decision to force heads of schools in Maharashtra to put up students to the Board examinations irrespective of their merits and not to detain them in the ninth standard. Tarkunde held that government's action was a gratuitous interference with the common law right of parents and heads of schools to educate children.

In another case, Tarkunde set aside the government's decision to ban a petty literary crossword competition conducted by the *Illustrated Weekly of India* on the ground that it was a game of chance. Tarkunde held that the competition was an exercise in skill. He believed the government was focusing its attention on small games when it was openly allowing gambling in horse racing. In both cases, the legal basis of his decisions was dubious and he overruled policies of government, but ultimately the government accepted both his decisions.

As a young junior lawyer I used to frequently appear in his court for the government. When I confronted the law against his views, Tarkunde had a favourite expression: "We shall find a way out." At that time, I deeply resented his judicial approach. In retrospect, I cannot say that Tarkunde was wrong.

The most abiding contribution of Tarkunde was his leadership and effort to safeguard secularism in India from religious intolerance. Strangely it came from a confirmed rationalist and agnostic. Tarkunde defended strongly the citizen's right to freedom of religion, conscience and religious practices. Two instances come to my mind.

In 1960, the Pope made his first ever visit abroad to inaugurate he Eucharistic Congress of Catholics in Bombay. The government made the Oval Maidan available to the Congress. The Government's action was challenged in court as aiding religion. The case came before Tarkunde. I was briefed to appear for the Cardinal with Nani Palkiwala. We feared that the case had come before an unsympathetic judge knowing Tarkunde's rationalist background. Our fears were misplaced. Tarkunde upheld the right of Catholics to hold the congress and the Government's help to them. He said that though India was a secular state it was not indifferent to religion.

Many years later in 1983 after his retirement, Tarkunde as a lawyer appeared for the Anand Margis in the Supreme Court to defend their religious beliefs to conduct processions in the streets of Calcutta with human skulls and daggers. His rationalist beliefs did not inhibit him to defend the rights of religious denominations even if such practices appeared to be bizarre to others. Despite his valiant efforts without any personal reward Tarkunde did not succeed.

Tarkunde rallied the forces of secularism amidst communal hatred. His was the voice of sanity which guided activists to confront the communal forces in the anti-Sikh riots in 1984, the Ayodhya outrage in 1092-1993 and the Gujarat carnage in 2002. One of his last writings in *Radical Humanist* was on the importance of the next national election to the secular fabric of our Constitution.

A great American judge, Oliver Wendell Holmes, once said that the intensity with which one does one's work was vital. He said an hour's intensity was worth many days of dragging work. Tarkunde had that intensity of approach in all that he did, whether he wrote a judgment, argued a case or espoused a national cause.

"The public life of India will be poorer by the loss of this man of commitment."

[From 'A People's Judge' by T R Andhyarujina *The Hindu*, April 11, 2004]

Discussion

A tribute is one wherein you shower encomium lavishly on a person either in speech or writing on an occasion. The occasion can be a happy one like someone receiving an award or honour/title or the day of superannuating or a sad occasion like death.

The above tribute started with a note on the death of Tarkunde. It indicates the occasion on which it is written. Next, the writer introduces Tarkunde and other organisations with which he was associated like Radical Democratic Party and his fields of interest like Citizens for Democracy etc. Later the writer deals with Tarkunde's achievements as a judge. The writer showers praise on Tarkunde as an unparalleled judge who was ready even to bend certain facts or law to deliver judgement which he considered just. The writer also illustrates the various occasions wherein Tarkunde upheld his belief in secularism and the practice of rational thinking. At the end also, the writer expresses his admiration for Tarkunde revealing the latter's intensity of approach in dealing with law and says that the country became poorer by the loss of such a great man of commitment. Here the writer chose not to write about the personal life of Tarkunde but his contribution at large to the society as a judge.

C. Short-biography

Example

Sir Alexander Fleming (1881-1955)
Alexander Fleming is remembered by scientists and non-scientists alike, all over the world, as the one who discovered Penicillin, which later became a basis for many other antibiotics. He was knighted in 1944 and received the Nobel Prize for Physiology or Medicine in 1945. The life-story of Fleming is very interesting to find the circumstances wherein he discovered Penicillin.

Alexander Fleming, the British bacteriologist was born in Lochfield, Ayrshire (UK). He was the son of a farmer. After moving to London at the age of fourteen, he worked as a clerk in a shipping office before enrolling himself, to study at St Mary Hospital in 1902. After being qualified, he joined the Inoculation Department under Almoroth Wright in 1906. Later in 1921, Fleming became assistant director. In no time Fleming gained expertise in the treatment of bacterial diseases by using vaccines and Chemotherapy. During World War I, Fleming and Wright served in Military Hospital and made advances in antiseptics for dressing wounds. In 1921, Fleming discovered 'lysozyne', a bacterial enzyme found in mucus, tears, blood server etc.

Only in 1928, Fleming made a major discovery in the field of bacteria. He noticed a contaminant mould growing in a culture dish containing 'staaphylococco' bacteria, which kills bacteria in the surrounding area. He identified the mould as 'Penicillin notatum' and the antibacterial substance it contained was called 'penicillin' by him.

Fleming, further demonstrated penicillin's effectiveness against many other pathogenic bacterias and its low toxicity. Thereafter, in 1940 Ernest Chain and Howard Florey proved its enormous value as an antibiotic. Their work paved the way for numerous other antibiotics and a revolution in the treatment of diseases.

[Adapted from *Longman Dictionary of Twentieth Century Biography* Pub: England: Longman 1985, P.174.]

Discussion

As you observed above, a short-biography does not deal with any praise unlike the tribute but deals with facts of life like education and career etc. In the above account, the writer deals with a short account of Fleming's life, education, and the beginning of his career and finally his discovery of Penicillin in a chronological order in detail. Besides, the writer gives the contribution of Fleming in the field of antibiotics and how the discovery of penicillin led to other developments and helped in treating bacterial diseases. The account gave in the beginning itself, his honours/title of Knighthood bestowed on him and the receipt of Nobel Prize by Fleming.

If you study all the three — profile/sketch, tribute and short-biography as a whole, you find certain common factors between them and a few differences too. No doubt, all these three deal with the accounts of people in a descriptive way. Among all of them, tribute is different mainly in expressing praise or admiration on the person while giving a sketch of life and professional profile of the person and awards. A profile gives all these and may give a critical evaluation of the person. Short-biography gives the personal profile in chronological order which is not a must with regard to a tribute. The importance of a short-biography is in giving factual account of the person dealing with all aspects of one's life.

Exercises

1. Read the following text. And fill in the columns in the table below.

> While thus chatting with two of them I became aware of the slightly built girl hiding behind the settee*. She must have been about eight, and was sweet and charming like her mother. Her hair was closely cropped, with a straight fringe across the forehead, in Chinese fashion. She was in jeans and in her half-sleeved loose jersey♦ and high boots, looked a miniature jungle queen. But she was behaving a bit too timidly, for one and was trying to avoid one.

Age	Overall Appearance (How does she look like)	Resembles whom?	Hair (Hair Style)	Dress	Personality (bold, dashing/timid etc)	Fat/lean (body - built)
—	—	—	—	—	—	—

2. Your elder brother sends you to the airport to receive a friend of his and sends an e-mail giving details about you to recognise you at the airport without any difficulty.

Give a description about yourself, as if given by your brother. You may begin like this:

Dear Mr Verma,
Please excuse me for not receiving you at the airport. I have to attend to an interview in the city just at that time when you arrive here.

---

* long soft seat with back and arms
♦ loose fitting knitted garment worn on a shirt or a blouse

Anyway my younger brother Krishna is going to receive you. You can easily recognise him. He is tall _____
_____
_____

(Complete it)

3. (Pair Work) Read and discuss the given outline below, with your partner, and do as directed.
Introduce Ms Sonalika Sahay, who would like to be an actor, to the Director, 'Glamour World Acting Academy', Delhi, through a letter, based on the outline given below:

Ms Sonalika Sahay ——wish to get training — to act in films. Aged 23 ——lean shoulder, tall 5-6" ——complexion ——eyes. Very charming, ——nose, ——hair, ——— hard working, ——chiselled features. ——willed and confident.

Career History: Short-listed for Fashion Week 2004, worked as air hostess in Singapore Airlines for 3 years. Worked for Nestle, Clinique & Ponds ads and walked the ramp for Raghavendra Rathore and a few more.

[From *India Today* March, 29, 2004]

Describing People

4. (Pair Work)

Read and discuss the given outline, with your partner and write a description of a beggar adding some more details:

Standing before —a shop – face wrinkled like a parchment. Piteous expression. A brown coarse —— cloak hung — on his right shoulders — thick-patched boots —— rough stick in the one hand — and a hat for alms —— in another hand.

(Taken from *Short Stories of Yesterday and Today*, Edited by Shiv K Kumar, 1978; OUP, 1992, P. 2-3)

5. (Pair Work)

Read the following text. Discuss with your partner about the personality of Rahim Khan and together write a few lines about Khan (a pen picture) giving particulars of age, mental disposition and profession of Khan.

> The Sun was setting behind the mango grove which fringed the western extremity of the village when Rahim Khan returned from the fields. Broad and strong despite his fifty odd years, with the plough on his shoulders, and driving his two oxen, he walked through the main street of village with a haughty and unfriendly air. As he approached the *chaupal* where a dozen or so peasants were collected for their evening smoke, the hilarious tones of gossip died down to cautious whispers. It was only when he had vanished round the corner and the heavy tread of his footsteps was heard no more that Kallu, passing the communal hookah to another, remarked, 'There goes the hard-hearted devil!' To which Nanah, the fat sweet-seller, added: 'He is getting worse and worse every day'.

[From *Twenty – Short Stories* Edited by Aban T. Bhatia & P.S. Mathur, 1976; Delhi, OUP, 1981, P. 88

6. Read the details and prepare an obituary note.

Name : Ustad Vilayat Khan (1928 — March 2004)

A great sitar artist who (carry) tradition forward —(make) significant innovations (died) recently (March 4). Introduced — 'singing sitar style' — an innovator and never (compromise) with tradition. —— (not like) mixing East and West in music . A rebel

(refuse) prestigious awards — A man (disturb) by lack of policy by the government of India —— a true musician,

[From *India Today,* March 29, 2004]

7. Read the following newspaper report. Imagine you are Mahendra Singh, the pillion rider who witnessed the road accident. Prepare the eyewitness account, to submit it to the officer concerned:

> **Dies in a mishap**
>
> Twenty-four year old, Avatar Singh, who was riding a motorcycle, died on the spot when a speeding lorry hit his vehicle from the rear on the Ring road, near Attapur crossroads on Saturday.
>
> His friend, Mahender Singh, who was pillion riding escaped with injuries. The mishap occurred at 4.30. a.m. when the duo, residents of Sikh Chawni at Kisenbagh were on their way to perform 'Prabhat Pheri' as part of Baisakhi festival. The Rajendranagar police registered a case.

8. (Profile/sketch/Tribute/Short-biography)

Read the following Tribute and do the two exercises that follow:

Dewang Mehata

The government of India and the IT sector owe a lot to the late Dewang Mehata. Mehata left the world when the country needed him most. It's the unkindest cut of all. The cruel fate nipped him when he was at the prime of his life and glory. He was the driving force behind the IT revolution in India. Being a strong optimist Mehata cherished the dream of seeing India as the next superpower in IT. (Para 1)

Mehata's life makes a fascinating study even to a common man besides the people in the field of IT. His life ran in a zigzag fashion from one field to the other with myriad colours. It was in 1983 when he was busy making documentary films his attention was drawn towards computers. He was in England in connection with 'Glimpses of India'—a documentary film that had won him awards. He realised the immense value of computer graphics and techno backed creativity when he was making the film. This motivated him to join in Imperial college, London, to do a course in computer graphics. (Para 2)

Mehata had a checkered career before he joined in Nasscom. He was an employee of Orissa Cements till Harish Mehata, an industry veteran, offered him a post in Nasscom.

Later, as the president of Nasscom, Mehata did his best to build the global brand equity of Indian software industry. He was the one who spread the slogan *'Roti, kapada, makaan, bijli, and bandwidth'* which indicate the requirements of the emerging twentieth century India. (Para3)

Mehata was a great workaholic and possessed an inherent skill in exerting influence on others. No matter who was in power, Mehata influenced the right people in power and always got special treatment for software. He could get many tax exemptions for software exports. He was responsible to a great extent for most of the decisions taken by the government of India regarding IT and shaping its policy in the sector. He was also the main cop who fought software piracy with a missionary zeal. Due to his efforts for the first time the word, 'cyber crime' entered the legal lexicon. He was not at all distressed by the economic slowdown in the US. Instead he felt that the slowdown was an opportunity to India for getting certain US companies outsourced. (Para 4)

It is difficult to list out the innumerable awards given to Mehata. He was awarded the 'IT man of the year' by the Dataquest and Computer World magazine named him as the 'Software Evangelist of the Year' for three consecutive years. In September 2000, Ernest and Young presented him with the 'Entrepreneur of the Year' award. Later that year the World Economic Forum listed him among the '100 Global Leaders of Tomorrow'. Mehata wrote extensively on subjects like politics, economics, software and Internet and organised more than 100 international seminars around the world. (Para 5)

Mehata was one of those great people of 'unfulfilled renown' who met their death when very young. April 13, 2001 was one of the darkest days in history when he died, at the age of 39, in a hotel suite in Sydney, Australia. With Dewang Mehata's death Nasscom has lost a visionary and the nation still mourns the loss of the most enthusiastic business campaigner. (Para 6)

[Adapted from 'A Man who defied Conventions' *The Hindu* May 1, 2001]

Now do the Exercises:

A. Match the following summary of a paragraph with the relevant paragraph number:

Summary of the - Paragraph	*Paragraph number*
The contribution of Mehata	Third paragraph
Awards	Second paragraph
The zigzag career of Mehata	First paragraph
Mehata before he specialised in software or IT	Fourth paragraph

B. Which of the words would you pick up most to include in the personality of Dewang Mehata? Put a tick mark [✓] or [5] before the word.

i) Proud, [ ] ii) optimistic [ ] iii) great enthusiast [ ] iv) a man of missionary zeal, [ ] v) workaholic [ ] vi) rebelling [ ] vii) skilled in influencing people [ ] viii) go-getter [ ]

9. Read the following data and write a short-biography of Kalpana Chawla, if you want you may add some more information (not more than 300 words):

- First Indian-American woman in space, after Rakesh Sharma who flew on Soviet Mission, Naturalised American citizen
- Born on July 1, 1961, in Karnal, Haryana, India
- Education, graduated from the Tagore School in Karnal in 1976, and B S in Aeronautical Engineering College in 1982. Shifted to the US and did her MS in Aeronautical Engineering in 1984 from University of Texas; and Ph D in Aerospace Engineering from the University of Colorado in 1988
- Marriage — with a Frenchman, Jean-Pierre Harrison, a freelance flying instructor
- Loved — flying aerobatics, hiking, back-packing and reading
- Career— started work in 1988 at NASA in the area of powered-lift computational fluid dynamics
- One of those 7 astronauts killed — in the space shuttle of Columbia, Feb 1, 2003 at the age of 41
- NASA's new supercomputer, SGI (r) Altix (tm) 3000 dedicated and named after Kalpana Chawla on Aug 4, 2004.

*****

II
Writing a Proposal

When you join the workforce in a company or organisation, you have to fulfil many duties. It is not simply doing the assigned work or a project and show results. Another facet begins– – maintaining work schedules, taking up projects, giving presentations, and making *proposals*. When you take up a project you have to submit a proposal and present it to the officer concerned for approval. The approval by the officer concerned depends upon many factors. One among such factors is the financial implications, the time factor, planning and discussions with the experts in the field. Your proposal will be very crucial and a basis for financial sanction and others. Then what is a proposal?

In every field of work, academic, administration, business, social or even personal life, one will have the experience of making a proposal. Some writers call it 'Proposal Reports.' It is something like a launching pad or springboard from where one jumps into action. Everyone should have a proposal before s/he embarks on a project. Proposal is something like a suggestion in a written mode or plan to be put into practice for the best interests of the company. In fact, it is a document (plan) that attempts to persuade someone to do something in everyone's best interests and it is submitted to the management or the sanctioning authority to be approved. Without the proposal nothing can be achieved in real terms. No building can be constructed without a blueprint or a model or a meeting without an agenda. If you want to build a house you cannot build it in the air. You should have a plan prepared by an architect and should have the cost estimation roughly. The same thing is done for any other project. It is, in other words, 'a specialised form of recommendation report'.* The difference between a general report and a proposal is that the former tells us what (work) was done and the latter tells us what (work) one is going to do and her/his plan of action. A perfect proposal tells the sanctioning officer what is required in terms of men, money and materials. It is nothing but a plan or design which reveals how a project will be executed. It is a tool in the hands of the management to decide whether to sanction a project or not. But all proposals may not involve money. For example, some proposals suggest change of policy or just to take an appropriate action. Or a proposal can be made for leave of absence for a faculty member to do research.

Generally, a proposal can be explained in terms of *problem and solution*. The problem can be any work, to be done and the solution is a plan which is presented in the form of a proposal. If it is a technical proposal, Gordon Mills says, "it solves a technical problem in a particular way, under a specified plan of management, for a specified sum of money"* Proposals can be short or long. And may be prepared by a single author (person) or group of authors or a committee. If there is more than one author, there will be an editor in that case. Proposals, concerned with large projects are the work of a team of authors. Similarly, the proposal may be as short as a single page or simply a letter. A proposal should be presented logically and clearly as it affects the performance of the company or individual. It generally includes, design, management and cost details.

1. The first one is *design*. It is nothing but a layout or plan proposed, as revealed already. As the name suggests, it gives step by step planning from the beginning to the end or it may have a flow chart or any graphic design. And you may call it a *design proposal*.

---

* *Technical Writing* by Gordon H. Mills & John A. Walter, 1962; New York: Holt Rinehart and Winston, 1978, P. 274.
* *Technical Writing* P.274

2. *Management.* It states how the entire project will be managed or executed with time schedules for completion, with quality assurance and can be called *management proposal.*
3. *Cost proposal.* It gives detailed estimation of costs in terms of labour and materials. Though a proposal contains these three basic elements but the entire document may be very long and it will be evaluated by experts in the field, like an engineer or a lawyer and their reports will be taken into account before the authority sanctions a proposal. The sanctioning authority requires certain information and solid details before it gives sanction. These factors emphasise how important a proposal is to start a project and the results of any project depend on a sound proposal. Obviously, a poorly presented proposal fails to get a contract or deal and brings losses to the company.

If the proposal happens to be, a big technical proposal, it involves many people like coordinator, evaluation team and legal committee. Then think of what kind of proposals you generally find.

Kinds of Proposals

Proposals are of two kinds *1. Technical 2. Non-Technical.*

2. 1 *Technical*

A technical proposal, as the name suggests, is purely technical in nature and is used in science, engineering, industries and information technology. It has certain characteristics like having special style and diction and contains certain graphics such as sketches, charts and graphs. Further, it has a scientific point of view and is objective in nature while presenting facts. Technical proposals are meant for a specific reader or group of readers, perhaps the staff of a certain research group, rather than for a great mass of readers*. For this reason the chapter confines itself to non-technical proposal.

---

* *Technical Writing* P.274

2.2 Non-Technical

Non-technical proposals are used in the fields connected with general, social, individual or administrative activities. This chapter deals with non-technical proposals only as the book aims at the general readers and their requirements.

Why a Proposal?
- Serves as a basis for taking a decision to start a project.
- Helps as a reference material or document to be read by experts concerned for giving opinions.
- Provides an evidence of work to be executed.
- Gives step by step planning for the execution of the project.
- Enhances the prestige of the company.

What goes into a Proposal?
It contains three stages basically— Planning, Designing and Estimating
1. Making a preliminary study 2. Developing a plan or outline 3. Writing a rough draft 4. Reviewing and revising 5. Cost estimation or proposal evaluation (in the case of some big Projects)

There is no universally accepted format or method of writing a proposal for a big or concise project. What is required is a well-written plan or layout which should direct the organisers or the company to carry out the project with an idea about the number of people needed, the design, and the total cost estimated to carryout the project. However, a format is suggested below for any general, non-technical project —

I *Introduction*
    A. Statement of the problem
    B. Summary of the proposed plan

II *Discussion of the Proposal*

III *Management Plan*
    A. Organisation
    B. Personnel

IV *Cost Analysis*

Note: All the titles may not be used for all kinds of proposals. You have to use discretion.

Or you may think of another format with other set of titles like–
1. *Introduction*
2. *Body*
3. *Conclusion*
4. *Budget*
5. *Documentation* **(where required)***

1. *Introduction.* This section deals with an overview or background and sets the stage for the proposal which is going to be dealt with shortly. 2. *Body* supplies the details of what is proposed and justification for the proposal. 3. *Conclusion* builds up an argument or justification to accept the proposal. 4. *Budget* It shows the amount of money needed to implement the proposal in detail for each phase for each thing step by step. 5. *Documentation* It supports the body of the proposal and provides materials in support of proposals.

How should be the language and tone?

- Use persuasive language and tone.
- Show how your proposal is cost effective.
- Adopt a confident tone.
- Deal with long and short-term benefits.
- Keep in your mind what the sanctioning authority wants from you.
- Guess the possible objections of the officer concerned.

The author takes up the former design — I Introduction II Discussion of the proposal, III Management plan, IV Cost analysis as a matter of convenience and suitability.

Let us consider the most familiar example of Tree plantation programme in a colony.

Example 1

Imagine you are the secretary of the MVS colony and the members of the colony decided to have a plantation programme to make their colony look more cool, green and attractive. The president of

---

* 'Proposals That Work', from *Improving Writing Skills,* by Arthur Asa Berger, New Delhi: Sage Publications, 1993, P.33

the colony asked the secretary to prepare a proposal for the Tree plantation giving cost estimation and other details to get the approval of the Executive Council.

Duration of the Work— 10 days: from 12 to 21st July 2004.
Timings: 10.30 a.m. to 5.30.p.m.
Estimated Cost: Cost Rs. 20, 000/ (Appr) Rs 1500 per month – recurring expenditure, later

I *Introduction*

The MVS colony is a newly developed one and situated on the outskirts of the city in a sprawling 4 acres site, abetting national highway (NH) 5. On the East, there is Bay of Bengal, on the West some hillocks, on the north there is the growing the city of Vishakhapatnam, and on the South vast plains. There are about 500 houses in the colony and some are 2 or 3 storied. It has 33 main roads and 54 lanes. It has a small park to be developed still. According to the plan, saplings like banyan, neem, coconut, and casuarinas will be planted on each side of the main road. On the lanes, saplings like palm and lemon, citrus (amla) and flame of the forest will be planted.

A. Statement of the problem:

MVS colony would like to plant about ten thousand (10, 000) saplings in their colony to make the colony more cool, green and beautiful and to promote water harvesting.

B. Summary of the proposal

The members of the colony in the General body meeting decided to make their colony green, and clean and promote water harvesting. They want to utilise the recent incentives offered by the Horticulture department to supply saplings free of cost, for those who plant them in the colonies. In view of this, the president asks the secretary to prepare a proposal for the plantation programme.

II *Discussion*

Last week, encouraged by the incentives offered by the Horticulture department, the General Body and the Executive Council of the colony met separately and decided to take up the plantation programme. They made rough estimation of the costs and decided to meet it from the reserved funds of the society and also accept voluntary donations.

III *Management Plan*

Two committees are formed to facilitate smooth functioning of the work.

a. Plantation committee b. Watering and Maintenance committee with the secretary as the coordinator and supervisor of the entire programme.

A. Organisation

i. Before the work starts:
   a. One week before the work starts a request will be made to the director of Horticulture Department for the free delivery of 10,000 saplings for use.
   b. A similar request will be made to the chairman of the Water Works of the Corporation, to supply water through a tanker — 4 days
   c. Arrangements for 2 lorries for rent—1 for bringing the saplings and another to bring manure.
   d. Arrangements for hiring 20 labourers to work on daily wages.

ii. After work starts:

The work starts on July 12th around 10.00 a.m. Twenty labourers will be taken on daily wages for 10 days. The plants will be brought a day before from the department, on a hired lorry. Labourers work from July 12th to 21st (including Sunday) and from 10 a.m. to 5.30 p.m.

B. Personnel

(i) 10 members each of the Plantation and Watering committees supervise the programme.
(ii) 20 young volunteers of the colony render assistance to it.
(iii) 2 gardeners will be appointed, later on monthly basis to look after the plantations.

IV Cost Analysis

The following table gives the details—

Table 1
Cost proposal

S.No	Things	Cost	Gardeners	Saplings	Total Cost Rs.
1.	Transport Rent (Lorries) - 2	Rs. 500 x 2	2	10, 000	1, 000
2.	Labourers -20 Per head Rs. 80/	Rs.80/ Each For 10 days 20 x 800			16, 000
3.	Saplings	———		Ashoka, Neem, Palm, Lemon, Gulmohur Casurina, Banyan etc.,	1,000
4.	Water tankers for rent and miscellaneous				2,000
5.	Other expenses				Total= Rs 20, 000

Table 2
Plan of plants to be planted—

S. No	Name of the Road Main Road/lane	No	Name of the Tree	Number of saplings	Total
1.	Main Roads	33	Banyan, Coconut, Palm, Gulmohur Bamboo etc	60 on each side 60x2= 120	33x120 3, 960= 4,000 (Appr)
2.	Lanes	54	Neem, Casuarinas, Citrus, Palm etc.	50 on each side 54x100= 5,400	54x100 =5400 (Appr)

S. No	Name of the Road Main Road/lane	No	Name of the Tree	Number of saplings	Total
3.	In the park		300 saplings	200 may be spoiled. 100 kept for replacing if some are dead.	Total= 9,400 Park 300 May be spoiled = 200 Reserve 100 Total= 10,000

The above proposal was submitted by the Secretary for approval to the President of the colony.

Example 2

Let us study a proposal, given below, submitted by an assistant senior personnel officer to the officer concerned for approval, with regard to taking the badminton team of their office for coaching, to the stadium.

I *Introduction*

The committee headed by the general manager decided to send ICPSU (Inter Central Power Sector Undertaking)—badminton team for tournament from the Power Grid Corporation of India Ltd. A decision was also taken to send the players for practise to be given by a professional coach for 11 days and make necessary arrangements. The team undergoes practise in the morning about 1 (one) hour and 6 (six) hours in the evening in Mathura Nagar Indoor Stadium, for 11 days (from 11-02-2004 to 21-02-2004). For the purpose of taking the members of the team daily to the stadium, transport arrangements have to be made. A proposal is submitted by the officer, concerned in this regard.

A. Statement of the Problem

Transport arrangements have to be made for the players to take them to the stadium for 11 days for getting coaching and practise from a professional coach.

B. Summary of the Proposed Solution

Quotations from different travel agents have to be collected and examined. A suitable vehicle (a hired vehicle with 7 seater capacity) has to be engaged at a fair cost, after examining the quotations.

II *Management Plan*

A. Organisation

The senior assistant personal officer prepares the proposal and collects 3 quotations from various Travel companies asking basic rates for 12 hours duration and other details and submits it to the Deputy General Manager (Establishment) and gets the sanction from the officer concerned.

After the approval and sanction of the amount a hired jeep will be taken up to transport the team daily for the said period.
Time:
Morning: 8.00 a.m. to 9.00 a.m. and Evening: 3.00 to 9.00 p.m.

B. *Personnel:*

Team Players —— 6
Referee ——1
Helper ——1 Driver ——1

III Cost Analysis

Sl No:	Agency	Basic rate for 12 hours	Charges for extra km	Charges for extra hour	Driver's allowance
1.	M/s Rao Travels	Rs. 1350/- & 120 kms free	Rs. 6/-	Rs. 40/-	Rs.50/ above 12 hours Rs.60/-
2.	Maruti Travels	Rs. 1950/- for hours & 90 kms free	Rs. 9/-	Rs. 75/-	Rs. 100/ per day
3.	Cosy Cabs	Rs. 1584/- & 150 kms	Rs. 7/-	Rs. 90/-	Rs.50/- after 9.0 p.m.

As seen from the above, the rates quoted by M/s Rao Travels are found to be reasonable in comparison with the others. The financial implications to engage a hired Qualis (Non-A/C) on 12 hour basis for 10 days would cost 22, 400/Rs (approx.) including driver charges. This amount can be spent under the head of IPSU tournament under welfare expenses.

Example 3

Some proposals may not involve money at all but may suggest a change of policy or suitable action to be taken up for facilitating some benefits to the employees.

Here is an example below wherein a proposal is made to the Director to take a suitable action for the benefit of employees.

Read it:

Deputy general manager of Human Resources (HR) submits a proposal to director (Personnel) regarding exemption from payment of road tax, for life, on their vehicles used by power grid employees who have inter-state transfers.

I *Introduction*

It is a well-known fact that services of Power Grid employees are liable to be transferred anywhere in India. Whenever an employee is transferred, they are required to get 'No Objection Certificate' from the RTA from the place they worked previously. They have to apply new registration with RTA at the new place of posting and pay life tax for the remaining life of the vehicle.

A. Statement of the Problem

The employees of the Power Grid incur a lot of expenditure, inconvenience and long wait every time they are transferred to a new place. The procedure of re-registration of vehicle at a new place of posting on being transferred is quite cumbersome and takes a long time.

B. Summary of proposed solution

The HR department of the corporate can take up the issue and approach the road transport ministry, Government of Andhra Pradesh and get exemption from the life tax for the vehicles of employees of the Power Grid.

In this connection, it may be stated that it is pertinent to follow the example of the defense personnels who have got similar exemption from state authorities. The governments of Tamil Nadu and Karnataka have given exemption for the employees of Central Public Sector Organisations from life tax in their respective states.

II. Management Plan

Corporate HR department takes up an appropriate action and transact with road transport authority to get the Life tax exemption for Power Grid employees.

Exercises-1.

1. (Pair Work). *Study and discuss the outline given below with your partner and make a formal proposal.*

Mr. G. Prasanna Kumar, director of Green Corps, asks Mr P N Rao, Deputy manager to make a proposal to have an interactive session. Introduction and statement of the problem are given to help you. Complete the proposal:

Necessary details to use:

Date: July 10, 2004. **Time**: 10.30. to 1.30 and 2.30 to 4.30 p.m.
Venue: Institute of Engineers, Kahiratabad, Hyderabad, **Contact No**: —
Invitees: 200; Guest Speakers – 4
Cost Estimation: 5,000/Rs – shamiyana furniture hiring charges, Remuneration for guest speakers, refreshment for the invitees and participants and miscellaneous expenses.

I *Introduction*

Mr. W G Prasanna Kumar, director of National Green Corps (NGC), a non-governmental organisation, in association with the Energy Conservation Mission, decides to conduct an interactive session with principals of 200 schools in twin cities, to inculcate the spirit of energy conservation in and through the school education system. As part of the campaign, energy learning and practise sessions would be conducted for the students of NGC. Later the students of NGC would take up campaigns in a big way in selected schools, during the academic year.

A. Statement of the Problem

Young students in schools should get awareness that the electricity generated by various means— like water, coal or nuclear power must be conserved. The wastage of power results in wastage of precious environmental resources. The organisation would like to inculcate among students the habit of conserving power.

B. *Summary of the proposed solution:*
——— —————— [Complete it]

II *Management*

A. Organisation: ——— ——— ———

B. Personnel: ——— ——————— Time Schedules ———————Venue

IV Cost Analysis:

——————— ——— ——————— ———————

Complete the above.

Exercise-2: (Group Work) *Read the following and work together with your partners. The text contains all the main elements of a proposal; each one of you can take each element and do the needful.*

The Proposal— 'Grant of Merit Award for the children of Power Grid employees', *contains all elements like Introduction, Statement of the Problem, Summary of the Proposed Solution, Management Plan, Cost Estimation etc., all mixed. After reading the following text, break it into different elements of a traditional ordinary Proposal and give a table where necessary:*

Mr P Sasi Kumar, no. 31277, is junior engineer. Grade 1, in Khammam section. His son's name is R Nand Kumar, SSC, March 2003, got second position in the State list, and secured 99 marks, in mathematics. The amount of Merit Award to be sanctioned is – – Rs. 2000/. Power Grid Corporation has relevant rules and a provision to grant Merit Award for the children of the employees who get highest rank. The conditions are the employee, whose child is eligible for the Merit Award, should have completed one year service in the regular establishment of the company on the date of the publication of the results. And the employee should apply for the Merit Award of his child within 180 days from the date of announcement of the results. The senior Assistant Personal Officer prepares the proposal for the approval of the Deputy General Manager (HR).

Exercise-3:
You are the student secretary of Lady Shriram College, Delhi, and conducting blood donation camp for 2 days in your college. You give a proposal to the local secretary of the Red Cross Society, in your city, about the camp to be held in your college.

Exercise-4:
You are the vice president of the Employees Association of your branch office. One of the staff is going to be superannuated (retirement) next week. On this occasion, the president of the association asks you to prepare a proposal to hold a small function in your office. Your association has decided to give a gift and arrange a party. Prepare a proposal and submit it to the president of the association.

*****

III

Writing Reports*

Any adult, either a student or an employee in an organisation or institution, in their day to day academic, business or official life, writes reports on events, meetings, projects, business matters, experiments done in a laboratory or a survey undertaken. As companies and corporates grow due to the liberalised economy and open markets, there is a need for writing business reports. Though there is no particular format for how a report should be, there are certain norms and guidelines to be followed when one writes them. As reports are of various kinds depending upon the purpose and readers, they differ in their content and style and no single format fits for all of them. The best way is to develop your own format with the aim of conveying factual information clearly and briefly.

No doubt, reports play a vital role in the career of a young employee or businessman. One who is skilled in writing a good report has definitely an edge over others and is sure of going up the ladder in their career. This unit aims to help prospective employees and others to write some of the most common type of reports by exposing them to certain models and exercises.

What is a report then? *A report is a written account to convey some factual information briefly and clearly to someone concerned with a purpose.* Reports can be formal (like Newspaper reports, business reports, minutes of a meeting, reporting of experiments

---

* This is a taken from the author's book, *Paragraph to Essay Writing,* New Delhi: Sterling Publications Pvt. Ltd, 2003.

or a project report or a survey) or informal (like reports based on letters, phone dialogues or a message). A Report neither refers to the feelings of the writer nor deals with unnecessary details but gives an impersonal account with essential details on a particular subject or event.

Before writing a report, one must have a clear idea of three things – 1) the subject of the report 2) the person who needs the report (targeted readers) 3) the purpose for which the report is intended to.

A report has:
- Essential particulars (like place, date, time etc.) or relevant facts
- Impersonal voice and expository tone
- Orderly presentation
- Clarity and brevity

In this chapter you learn the following types of reports —
- Newspaper Reports
- Reports based on Interviews
- Business Reports (Based on a survey)
- Reporting of Experiments
- Reporting of Meetings (Minutes)

3.1 Newspaper Reports

Newspaper reports cover a wide variety of subjects like politics, administration, industry and commerce, sports, science and technology and many others.

Read the following reports:

> ### 1. MIG Crashes
> **SHIMLA, March 28,** A MIG-21 fighter aircraft of the Indian Air Force (IAF) crashed near Dhanga Pir, in Nurpur area of Kangra district, on Tuesday night during routine exercise, police sources said today. The pilot, who received injuries, was rushed to the IAF hospital —
> **PTI**

2. Solar Eclipse on June 21

MUMBAI, MARCH 28 The first total eclipse of the millennium will occur on June 21, this year, said Dr. Bhart Adur of Nehru Centre here. He will lead a 20 member experts team to Africa to witness this event. However, this eclipse will not be visible in India—

UNI

3. Nine Killed in a road mishap

By our correspondent
MAHABUBNAGAR, MARCH, 27

Nine persons were killed and three others *were* injured critically when the jeep by which they were traveling fell into a roadside ditch after being hit by a lorry at about 8. 30 p.m. on Tuesday at Shakapur village near Kothakota on the NH-7 in Mahabubnagar district.

The injured are *being treated* at the Government Headquarters Hospital in Mahabubnagar. According to information available, all those travelling in the jeep belonged to Mandakal mandal in Gadwal division and they were said to be returning to their village after attending a public meeting addressed by Venkaiah Naidu, Union Minister for Rural Development, at Jadcherla Town.

4. Clinton to visit Gujarat

NEW DELHI, MARCH 28. The former U.S. President, Mr. Bill Clinton, will undertake a week-long private visit to India, during which he will tour quake-affected areas in Gujarat and meet the Prime Minister and other leaders.

" We are extending all courtesies due to former heads of state," a Foreign Office spokesman told reporters on Mr Clinton's visit which comes a year after a highly successful Presidential one last March,—

PTI

Discussion:

You might have noticed *title, place* and *date* written in all the above reports. These three are the essential features of a newspaper report. The first line of the report expands the title and gives the summary of it. The purpose of the report is to publish it in the newspaper and the readers are the general public. The reporter gives the essential details only of an accident/event occurrence very briefly and clearly. The details include *when* a particular incident/event happened and *how* and *where* it happened and the *names of the people* connected with it and other essential facts.

In **Report 1,** the reporter gives the name of the flight; the place where it crashed and the day on which it occurred; the people injured and whether they are treated. Thus, all the essential details are given in an impersonal voice, clearly and briefly. Further, you might have noticed past tense in every sentence. As the incident was over in the past and reported much later, past tense is used invariably. In **Report 2**, all the details like the date when solar eclipse occurs, the name of the team which leads to Africa and the necessary information that it is not visible in India — are given. Here you don't find *past tense* as the incident refers to future. In **Report 3,** you get the essential details like the number of people killed; how the tragedy were occurred; the time of the tragedy (when); the place/location of the tragedy; whether the injured treated and the occasion of the tragedy. **Report 4** gives the details of the person (Mr. Bill Clinton) who visits India; duration of his visit; the places he intends to visit; the people whom he meets and whether courtesies will be extended to him etc.

Besides the essential details of the events, you notice certain expressions or words such as — 'police sources said' (Rpt.1); 'Dr Bharat Adur of Nehru Centre said' (Rpt. 2); 'According to information available' (Rpt.3); 'a Foreign Office spokesman told' (Rpt.4)'. All these words reveal the various sources from where the reporter collected the information and their authenticity.

Further, notice the verbs, in italics — *'was rushed'* (Rpt-1) *'were killed'*, *'were injured'*; *'are being treated'* (Rpt3) — all these verbs are in *Passive Voice*. You find very often-passive verbs when the doer is not important. But you find other tenses also when the report contains information about future events, as in the case of report no 2 and 4.

A Newspaper Report contains —
- A title
- Place and date
- First line expands the title
- Essential details of the incident
- Mentions the sources of information

EXERCISES:
1. *Suggest a title to the report given below and write it on the blank at the top of the report.*

———————————————————————— (Title)?

MUMBAI, MARCH 28. An overflying Gulf Air Boeing 767-300 flight was today diverted to Chhatrpati Shivaji international Airport here after a 'suspected article' was found on board the aircraft.

The cabin crew on board the flight from Dhaka to Abu Dhabi noticed a 'bag' near a door and informed the commander who sought permission to land here.

The bomb detection and disposal squad checked the bag and it was found to contain a 'wooden box' along with clothes. The 'box' has been placed in the cooling pit, the sources said.

There were 224 passengers and 12 crew on board the aircraft which was finally cleared at 3.20 p.m.- PTI.

2. *Find here 3 different reports on the same matter. Which of the following is the most satisfactory report based on the norms discussed above?*

---

a) Computerized Reservation System inaugurated

The General Manager, South Central Railway, Mr N.Krithivasan, on Tuesday, inaugurated a computerized passenger reservation system at the Tandur Railway Station in the adjoining Ranga Reddy district. A press release said, the facility was expected to benefit the 1.40-lakh local population in the industrial belt and also the people in the adjoining Gulbarga district of Karnataka State, covered by the Secunderabad division of SCR.

b) Computerized Reservation System inaugurated

HYDERABAD, MARCH 27. Lucky are the people of Tandur! The General Manager, South Central Railway, Mr. N.Krithivasan, on Tuesday, inaugurated a computerized passenger reservation system at the Tandur Railway Station in the adjoining Ranga Reddy district. A press release said, the facility was expected to benefit the 1.40 lakh local population in the industrial belt and also the people in the adjoining Gulbarga district of Karnataka State, covered by the Secunderabad division of SCR. My dream has been fulfilled at last.

c) Computerized Reservation System Inaugurated

HYDERABAD, MARCH 27.
The General Manager, South Central Railway, Mr N. Krithivasan, on Tuesday, inaugurated a computerized passenger reservation system at the Tandur Railway Station in the adjoining Ranga Reddy district. A press release said, the facility was expected to benefit the 1.40 lakh local population in the industrial belt and also the people in the adjoining Gulbarga district of Karnataka State, covered by the Secunderabad division of SCR.

3. *Here is a report, "P.T.Usha presented 'Woman Achiever' award" in four paragraphs. The paragraphs are not in the right order but jumbled up. Rewrite the report putting the paragraphs in the right order:*

P. T. Usha presented 'Woman Achiever' award

MUMBAI, APRIL 18. Receiving the honour, Usha announced the setting up of the Usha School of Athletics, saying it was her way of giving back to the nation what she had been receiving till now.

Professional management was of utmost importance in sports to produce world class athletes, the sprint queen said adding her academy would try to achieve this.

Golden girl of Indian athletics P.T. Usha was given this year's 'Woman Achiever' award for outstanding contribution in the field of sports by the ladies wing of the Indian Merchants' Chamber (MC) here on Wednesday.

The award was presented to Usha at the 23rd annual general meeting of the ladies wing of the IMC, which had a theme of Women Work Wonders (www.com) for the year.

4. Using the outlines given below, write a short newspaper report:
Torrential rain in Mumbai – began afternoon – office goers, students stranded – railway lines under water – road transport affected – residents move out of slumps – buses and lorries help stranded to reach home – holiday declared for tomorrow.

3.2 Reports Based on Interviews

In this section you learn and practise two kinds of reports – 1) *based on interviews* which are between two persons, a formal and traditional kind where there is no need of electronic media. You may be familiar with these kinds of interviews since long and it is a sort of off line conversation. The other is 2) *online chats* which have come into vogue since the rise of Internet users and cyber cafes.

The writer of a report has many sources on which s/he makes a report. A correspondent who reports on events/ accidents for a general reader gets the information for his/her report from the people who witnessed the incident (eyewitness accounts) or by interviewing the people concerned (as in the case of newspaper reports).

A reporter has other sources besides interviews like questionnaires, surveys, and published or unpublished records to write articles in the magazines or newspapers.

3.2.1 *General or traditional kind of interviews:*
Read the following:
The special correspondent of *The Hindu* who writes a regular column on sports to the paper, interviewed the parents and coaches of Mr Pullela Gopi Chand, winner of All England Badminton Championship, 2001.

Correspondent: Are you excited when you heard the news of your son when he won the All England Badminton Championship?
Subhas Chandra Bose: (Father): We're happy that he has been able to achieve this. I'm grateful for all those who are responsible for his success.

Cor: Would you like to mention anyone specially to thank for?

Mr Bose: Yes, I've to make a special mention of Dr. Ashok Raj Gopal who treated my son in 1993-94 when he had a serious injury and was bedridden for six months. It was a trying time for Gopi. Just now Dr. Raj Gopal called us up to congratulate on Gopi's success.

Cor: How do you feel Ma'm being the mother of Gopi Chand?

Mrs. Bose: Yes, I'm very very happy. I'm over joyed and feel proud of him.

Cor: Being a sister, Himabindu, how do you share your brother's joy?

Himabindu (Sister): Yes, very thrilled. My brother is a very focussed person. No movies, no parties. Even if he miss one practice match he considers it a big loss.

Cor: Mr Sachdev, How do you account his success, as a coach who knows him for 11 years (1985-96)?

Sachdev: He has done a wonderful job. I'm very happy. His was an authoritarian win.

He dictated terms throughout the tournament.

Cor: Mr Verma, do you consider your role, as President of BAI, is a major factor for his victory?

V.K. Verma: Yes, I played a considerable role, if I don't exaggerate. It was me who pushed him to BPL Academy which helped him to get international exposure.

Cor: Mr Padukone, what do you think the effect of Gopi Chand's victory on other upcoming players?

Padukone: I'm proud of him. This victory will provide confidence which the Indian players basically lack. Gopi has shown that Indians can do it.

[Mr Subhas Chandra Bose – father, Mrs Subbaravamma Bose – mother; Himabindu – sister; Mr Sanjiv Sachdeva – coach, from 1985-96; V.K. Verma, President (BAI- Badminton Association of India), Prakash Padukone – winner of All England Badminton Championship, 1980 and coach to Gopi at BPL-PBA Academy, Bangalore]

(Adapted from *The Hindu*, 12-03-2001)

Discussion: As it is a direct interview between the members of Gopi Chand's family and his coaches the whole talk is in a dialogue form with questions and answers. There may be some important and some unimportant questions. The whole dialogue is in *direct speech* and present tense. The dialogue (conversation) becomes a source or document to the reporter who prepares his/her report. The norms like clarity, brevity, objectivity and impersonal voice have to be followed here also, as in the case of a newspaper report. The reader and purpose of the report must be clear in the mind of the reporter before s/he prepares the report. The whole report should often be in indirect speech (reported speech) and past tense.

Example 1:
Write a report of the above interview to publish it in your college magazine, in 100-120 words:
[Note: your audience (readers) are staff and students of your college who are interested in sports and games]

Answer:
When Mr. Gopi Chand won the All England Badminton Championship, his parents, sister, Himabindu and his coaches were extremely happy and much thrilled at his success.

His father, Mr. Subhas Chandra Bose, Asst. General Manager, Indian Overseas Bank, expressed his gratitude to all those people who were responsible for his son's victory and especially to Dr. Ashok Rajgopal who treated Gopi in 1993-94 when he was injured. From the account of his sister, Himabindu, Gopi is a focussed man who would take his practice matches seriously and never miss them. One of the coaches Mr. Sanjiv Sachdev (Coach at Bangalore, 1985-96), felt that Gopi's victory was an authoritative win. Another coach, Mr. V.K. Verma, (President, BAI, New Delhi) played a considerable role in the career of Gopi by exposing him to the international scene. Mr. Padukone, winner of All England Badminton Championship in 1980 and Gopi's coach at BPL-PBA Academy, Bangalore, was confident that the victory of Gopi Chand would, certainly, boost the morale of the Indian players.

Writing Reports

Note: In the following pages you find another example of an interview with one person and on one topic, of the first kind.

2. Read the following text:
Here is an interview between Dilip Chhabria, CMD of DC-Trends [a car designing company], New Delhi and Mr. Vijay Pushkarana, correspondent of *The Week*:
[Dilip Chhabria has an ever-increasing passion for cars since he was a child. The passion has grown with him. He set up a company, DC Trends in 1981. He has designed about 450 cars in the last eight years, a world record. His company rebuilds everything except the vital parts. His initials have become a brand label for designer automobiles.]

VP: How did you come up with the idea of designer cars?
DC: I've been eating, sleeping, breathing and dreaming cars, since I was a toddler. So at least I am not surprised that I majored in auto-transportation design in California.
VP: When did you first come to India to do this business of car designing?
DC: Only in 1992, not knowing how the market would be I indulged myself into this business. The first car I did was a Maruti Gypsy, just to indulge my creative instincts. It was a runaway success and got mobbed wherever it was driven.
VP: What was your investment then, and how is your concern placed in terms of market and viability?
DC: I started off with Rs. 25 lakhs, and now we are worth Rs.25 crore. We have 450 regular employees.
VP: What kind of people work for you?
DC: There are some mechanics and many artisans. Like the artisans of Moradabad who hone their skills that have been passed down from generations, and these are the skills you need in the automotive industry, particularly in the design segment. It is simply marrying my education to their handcrafting skills.
VP: How about the market, is there enough to make it viable?
DC: The customised cars market depends on human aspirations, the urge to display exclusiveness. There are lots of young people who like my cars. So the market must be there. It is not a case of

mass production and assembly lines of cars rolling out by the minute. What we are doing is tough. Each car has to be worked, on over a long time.

VP: What keeps you going?

DC: The bottom line is that we are the only one of our kind in the organised sector. My cars and even I get mobbed. I receive about 400 fan letters daily, most of them youngsters who want to emulate me, and think it's all about money, glamour and creativity. I tell them that it's more about real hard work.

VP: What is your favourite car?

DC: My personal favourite is the Sierra Arya. The chassis and mechanism, are the same, everything else is different. But I also like the Mercedes Benz we designed for ourselves at our own cost and sent to Germany to participate in a show. We got rave reviews and feedback on that. It is a step forward for DC and India, because it is like selling ice to Eskimos.

VP: What is remarkable about your favourite car?

DC: It's a timeless car. It was done three-and-half years ago. You look at it today,
and you can't improve it, which means it's a classic, a great car.

VP: Do you have a presence out of India?

DC: We are global, in the sense many of our cars are on the roads in Europe and America. We'll also enter into strategic alliance with some Europe-based firms in a couple of months. DC designs have got world-class systems.

VP: Given your passion for cars, how come you did not get into the business of car manufacture?

VP: You need very deep pockets for that. Moreover, I am a designer, creative artist, rather than an industrialist.

[Adapted from 'We are One of a Kind' *The Week*, March 25, 2001]

Example 2:
Write a report of the above interview in 200-220 words to publish it in the magazine, 'Business Today'.
(Note: Your audience are businessmen who are interested in car designing, car manufacturing and prospective car owners and others

related with car business. The purpose of the report is to publish it in a business magazine.)

Answer:
(Dilip Chhabria, CMD of the 10-year-old company, DC Trends has set a world record by rolling out 450 design cars in the last eight years.)

Mr Chhabria has a passion for cars since he was a toddler and it has grown with him. He came back to India in 1981, after his studies in auto-transportation designs in California, to start a profitable business with his father's money. His first car design, Maruti Gypsy was a runaway success. He started his business with Rs 25 lakhs and now it is worth 25 crores. His education and designing skills are matched to the skills of artisans. He believes that there is a good market for his design segment.

DC Trends is the only one of its kind in the organised sector which keeps him going for some more years. The most sought after Mercedes Benz was designed by him to participate in a show. Many of his cars are on the roads of Europe and America and his company is going to enter into an alliance with Europe-based firm in a couple of months. In spite of all the success in design trends, he has no intention to enter into the manufacturing field. He wants to be a creative artist only.

3.2.2 Interviews in Online Chats:

What is a Chat?
You might have an experience of online chats of late, after the increase of cyber cafes and have watched video conferences in TV. Sometimes newspapers (*The Times of India*) publish some recorded chats between an artist, celebrity or well-known personality and a small group of people who take part in the chat. The difference between an interview (traditional kind) and a chat is considerably less. The former is more *formal* and the latter is *informal*. Conversation/dialogue is common in both the cases. The topic changes from question to question often in online chats, as a group of people take part in the chat. In a traditional interview, the

main topic will generally be the same and one person (the reporter) only puts questions. When you write a report based on a chat, you have to bring coherence and unity as in the interview of the first variety, by bridging the gap between one question and another or one topic to another.

Example:
Here is a recorded online chat between Sapna Mukherji, the popular playback singer, and others like Manu, Bela and others. Make a Report:

Q: You are a successful film playback singer, why have you ventured into Pop? – Manu

A: I am into both. I sing for movies and cut albums as well. I love playback singing. In albums you get total exposure, in movies there are limitations. However, I like both and have therefore ventured into both the arenas.

Q: Are you a trained classical singer and how does the classical training help? – Bela

A: I am not a trained classical singer. I had learnt little from my mom.
When I came to Mumbai Kalyanji-Anandji advised me to learn singing, so I did learn a little from them. But you need to know classical to do playback, and classical training has definitely helped me. You have to know the *raag,* notations and of course *riyaaz* is a must.

Q: Why a change in name from Sapna to Saapna? – Savy

A: For numerology sake.

Q: How does a female feel in the male dominated world? – Zena

A: For singers its not very male dominated.

Q: Which co-singer suits you the best? – Manu

A: I have sung with all singers. I think it goes with everyone. My first duet I sang with Kishoreda, and I can't ever forget that wonderful day in my life.

['Indiatimes Chat' *The Times of India,* Hyderabad, Oct 20, 2000.];

Discussion:

In the reports based on online chats also the direct speech in the dialogue changes into indirect speech and the tense also changes sometimes. For example, the sentence-'I love playback singing'- changes into 'she loves playback singing'. To bridge the gaps between one topic and another you have to use some transition words like 'confesses', 'believes' or 'hopes', or 'thinks' etc, according to the context. You have to bring clarity and brevity as in other reports.

Answer:

In one of the 'Indiatimes Chat' (online Chat) Saapna Mukherjee told some of the members in the chat that though she is a playback singer she loves to cut albums too. She loves both the fields. But the difference is that she gets total exposure in albums whereas there are certain limitations in playback singing. She confesses to them that she is not a trained classical singer but learnt a little on the advice of Kalyanji-Anandji. She believes that the classical training helped her definitely and she could learn the notations of various 'raagas'. On being questioned, she told them that she has changed her name from 'Sapna' to 'Saapna' for the sake of numerology. Her first duet was with Kishoreda and she thinks that her voice goes with everyone.

EXERCISES:

1. *Here is an interview of the principal of St George's Boys Grammar School by a student which got published in a newspaper. Read it and make a report of it:*

Mr. Dinesh: How do you feel being the principal of St George's Grammar School, the most prestigious one in the state?

Principal: It's been rewarding. It feels good to shape and mould children.

D: What is your principle, being a modern principal?

P: The school motto of course: *Perseverantia omnia vincit.* Perseverance conquers all things and my very personal principle is being honest. Absolute, total honesty.

D: Do you believe in punishing a child?

P: I do not look at it as a punishment. If anyone tries to harm another child, or damage property, I draw the line right there. I feel every child has a right to feel secure and if anyone tries to fool around with that, he needs to be disciplined so, I call it disciplining a child, rather than punishing.

D: What is the one thing you would like to change around you?

P: I wish there was more order, followed by cleanliness. Order helps in learning.

D: Do you believe this because you are from a military background?

P: No, not exactly.

D: So you think there is a lot of pressure on students due to our education system?

P: Yes, there is a lot of pressure. It's due to an explosion of knowledge. There is a lot of competition; definitely a lot more than there was in our times. But some amount of pressure is needed to egg you on. The pressure must come from within and not from outside. One must yearn to excel and be on top. That should be your driving force and motivation, not external pressure.

D: What do you feel about schools denying children their hall tickets just before their public exams?

P: I feel every child has a right to write his/her public examination. Some children need to be given chances, while some do not deserve chances.

D: But a year is wasted, right?

P: Where is the question of wasting a year, where 8 to 9 months have already been wasted. Some children are late bloomers, but some do not work hard at all. I think the latter group does not deserve a chance.

D: What would you say, to sum it all up?

P: Being a teacher gives me a great feeling. Just the thought of being able to influence generations, makes all the work worthwhile. This profession is extremely rewarding.

[Adapted from 'A Principal with principles' by Vishal Gupta, Std XI 'Young World' *The Hindu,* June 9th, 2001]

2. *Here is an online chat between the famous cricket player, Dilip Vengsarkar and the members. Read the dialogue between him and the members and make a report:*

'Cricket can help build bridges with Pakistan'
– Dilip Vengsarkar

Q: Will the outcome of the Agra summit have any effect on Indo-Pak cricket? – V

A: It will surely have a positive effect on Indo Pak cricket. It was important to have a dialogue between the two nations, in order to get rid of the mistrusts and lack of confidence in each other.

Q: Do you think cricket can help build bridges with Pakistan? – I

A: Definitely. When we played the test series against Pakistan in 1986 in India, there was lot of tension on the border. General Zia himself came to Jaipur to watch the test and in way diffused tension.

Q: What kind of feeling does the Indian team undergo while playing against Pakistan? – Shail

A: We have been traditional rivals for years together and hence, both the teams try to give their best in a match. But definitely, there is no feeling of hatred. Rather, the competitive spirits run very high when we play with each other.

['Indiatimes Chat' *The Times of India*, July 18, 2001]

3.3 Business Reports

You have already come a long way with enough knowledge and practice in writing a few kinds of reports. In this section, you are going to learn and practise a few varieties of *Business Reports* which help you in business, administrative or academic careers. Business reports differ widely from other reports like newspaper reports, recommendation reports, reports based on interviews and reports of science experiments and others. In spite of certain differences between each two, there will be certain common factors like representing the facts clearly and briefly, giving essential details and using impersonal voice etc. At the same time, each kind of report has its own unique basic format.

Why do you need a business report?

As companies and corporates grow, after the liberalised economy and open markets, the need for writing business reports increases day-by-day. With the growth of administrative, or other establishments, the need to write reports increases. Business reports need not be about trade and commerce only but can be in any field. No employee or employer can escape the duty of writing a report when s/he finishes any work, project or survey or before taking a decision. The need for effective reports is so much that many large establishments and corporations have set up *Editorial Departments* to supervise the production of reports submitted by their staff. Persons with the required skills of report writing obviously have an advantage over others who lack them.

Think of these questions—
- What is a business report?
- Who reads a report?
- What makes a good report?
- Kinds of reports & how to write

What is a business report?

Like other reports, a business report too gives factual, essential and relevant information on a piece of work done, survey conducted, progress shown, a tour undertaken, a meeting/conference held, or any other assignment done. These business reports are based on the work experience, direct observation, survey, interviews, questionnaires or published/unpublished materials. Reports are not meant for amusement, to entertain or educate the readers. But, in fact, they are meant for a specific purpose and for a particular reader to assess the work done by a person or to get feed back on a particular matter. These reports facilitate the work s/he is doing and get a kind of feed back before one takes a decision. Whatever the kind of work a person does, at the end of it, the employer asks the employee to write a report of one sort or the other in one context or the other. So no work means no report.

Who reads a report?

Every report has two kinds of readers. One is the *primary* or *special reader* and the other is the *secondary reader*. In any case, no report is meant for the general reader. The primary reader is the person to whom the report is specifically addressed or the person who asked the report to make and is stated on the title page like 'To Mr. B.R. Sinha, chief executive officer or managing director' etc. Secondary readers are the persons who may need to refer to this report at a later time for reference or other purposes. The primary reader is generally some executive who needs the report and the one who commissioned a member or committee to prepare a report before s/he takes an administrative decision.

A good report writer is one —
- Who states and analyses the problem clearly and briefly.
- Who looks for relevant evidence or sources.
- Who adopts expository and objective tone instead of a persuasive one.
- Who relies on verifiable evidence for his/her report.
- Who responds to the needs of the primary reader and their concerns.
- Who makes his/her report worth of the readers' time.

A few kinds of business reports:
- Periodic reports (Monthly, quarterly or annual reports)
- Work reports (after completion of a work or event)
- Investigative reports
- Recommendation reports (based on a survey)
- Search for causes

Note: *A business report can be in the form of a semi-formal letter too. But it is generally in the form of a formal report containing the elements such as title, terms of reference and proceedings etc.*

In this unit, you learn and practise two kinds of business reports – **1. Recommendation reports** (based on a survey) and **2. Single work reports** (information reports) which are essential in any career.

3.3.1 Recommendation Reports:

Before you prepare a recommendation report think of the following:
- The purpose of the report or why the report.
- Who commissioned your report (Part of Terms of Reference).
- The date of submission of your report.
- The needs of your readers - (or primary reader)
- Make the report clear, brief and objective.
- Collect data/information through a survey, questionnaire, interviews or any other suitable means.
- Select a format to suit your purpose.
- Check whether you need a summary, tables, charts etc.
- Prove that your report is worth of your readers' time.
- Better to prepare a *brief* before you start a report.

As stated above, before you make any *recommendation report* or start a survey, you should have a brief before you, to know the details of terms of reference. The brief gives more clarity to the primary reader of the report as well as to the others but many reports may not contain it.

Example:
Read the following report:

Brief:

> From: **Zonal Manager** (sales)
> To : **Regional Sales Supervisor**
> Please make a survey of the customer attitude towards Tomato Glow toilet soap of Rodrej Company Ltd. in Andhra Pradesh Region and record their appreciation or complaints and their suggestions. Based on the survey, you can make a few recommendations for the improvement of the product and thereby increase the sales. The report is to be presented before the next board of directors meet to be held on Sept.20th.

Title: Survey of customer attitude of Tomato Glow toilet soap in Andhra Pradesh region.

Terms of Reference:
The Regional Sales Supervisor of Andhra Pradesh is requested to undertake a survey and submit a report to the zonal manager, to

improve the sales and put it before the next board of directors meet to be held on September 20, 2001.

Proceedings:
Based on the questionnaire circulated to 3,700 customers in various towns and about 50 or 60 direct interviews conducted in major towns, it is clear that a majority of the customers have been satisfied with Tomato Glow soap with some reservations.

Findings:
1. 40% of the toilet soap users of Andhra Pradesh region have been using the Tomato Glow soap, as revealed from a random sample survey.
2. 70% of those who are using it, liked the soap for its tomato flavour, sweet fragrance and light lavender colour. But they expressed dissatisfaction for the reason that it costs high, i.e., Rs 18.
3. Nearly 40% of the users complained that the soap doesn't have strong fragrance which can be smelt from a long distance. Secondly, they complain that the soap doesn't yield enough lather and dissolves easily. Besides, they want the soap to last longer instead of 'being melted' after a few days of use.
4. They find that the packaging of the soap is not convenient to pick and carry in travels.
5. 30% of the customers wished for a choice of colours, sizes and weight.

Conclusions:
1. The product Tomato Glow toilet soap has been well-received and acclaimed mostly by the upper and lower-middle class people in big towns and the youth, mostly the student community, for the novelty of its colour and fragrance. It is the second most popular one after Lux toilet soap.
2. The product should be continued by reducing the price a little and with a choice of colours, shapes and weight with an attractive package.

Recommendations:

a) In view of the findings based on the survey and direct interviews conducted, I recommend that certain changes have to be brought in before the next product comes.
b) The cost of the product should be reduced slightly without changing the present weight.
c) The product should be available in different shapes like round, square, rectangular instead of the stereotyped oval shape.
d) The product can be available in various pleasant colours, instead of the same lavender colour always, like light green, cream or light blue.
e) The quality of the packaging material also can be improved.
f) The reasons for the dissatisfaction of the customers should be investigated by the Research and Analysis wing.

Discussion:

In the above example, you might have observed a brief which is followed by the report. The brief is something like the agenda which is needed to prepare the minutes of a meeting (which you are going to learn shortly). It gives you the required information such as the person who commissioned the report, who writes the report, the intended purpose and the date before which the report should be submitted etc. These details are called terms of reference. When a brief is not given, better you prepare one, to have a clear idea of the purpose of a report and the person who commissioned the report and other details. Title, terms of reference, proceedings, findings, conclusions, and recommendations are the main elements of any recommendation report (based on a survey). In some reports like work reports or information reports, you do not find recommendations but have the other elements. You have to make recommendations only when you are asked to. To support your findings sometimes you may have to provide tables or charts. A report can be made on any topic. Almost all kinds of reports which have a supporting data, generally have conclusions. Conclusions are personal statements made by the reporter based on the findings, which are in turn based on the data or survey undertaken.

3.3.2. Work Reports and Reporting of Events:

Work reports are those written at the end of your work or an event meant to convey information or analysis. Even young students may be asked to write reports by their teacher on an educational tour, a school function, or scout camp to publish it in the school magazine or as part of a home assignment. Or any faculty member, at the end of an official tour or a conference attended to, will be asked to write a report on it, after s/he returns. All these reports can be called Work Reports or Reporting of Events *(based on experience)*.

Example:

Read the following report:

A World Sanskrit Conference was organised by the Ministry of Human Resource Development, at the Vigyan Bhavan, New Delhi, from April 5th to 9th, 2001, with a view to promote Sanskrit studies and research in general and to exchange ideas among the scholars in India and abroad. The conference was inaugurated by Prime Minister Atal Behari Vajpai, with a special address by the renowned German scholar, Dr Frederick Wilhelm, on April 5, 2001.

Around 900 delegates attended the conference and presented papers on different topics varying from Vedas, literature, Saastras (Sciences) to current topics such as ecology and environment and information technology. The delegates presented papers in Hindi, Sanskrit and English. In the science section, botany, quantum mechanics, AIDS, epilepsy, ayurveda and ecology and environment were some of the subjects discussed with productive perspectives. The influence of Sanskrit on Indian and other world languages was traced by some of the participants in their papers. Considerable emphasis was given to rare unpublished manuscripts scattered all over the world and the need to catalogue them was stressed by Dr Kapila Vatsayana in her key note address. Some of the scholars showed their concern on the current issues like human rights and preservation of wildlife bio-diversity in their papers like 'Human Rights in Sanskrit Textual Sources' and 'Role of Sanskrit in Preservation of Wildlife', 'Bio-diversity and Environment'.

The scholars were provided entertainment too through 'Kavi Sammelan', dance, music and drama from various parts of India.

The valedictory speech by the former President Mr R Venkat Raman and Dr Karan Singh's special address provided the right concluding note to the conference.

[Adapted from – 'World Sanskrit Conference' *The Hindu*, May 8, 2001]

Discussion:
Like other reports, work reports/reporting of events too must be concise and only the relevant information should be included. Elaborate explanations and irrelevant details are left out. The above report gives the details such as the person who inaugurated, the organisation who sponsored, the date and duration of the conference, the number of delegates who attended to, the number of papers presented by and other essential details only, are given. The tone of the report is impersonal and objective. The style is very formal and goes as in a matter of fact narration. Each paragraph deals with one aspect of the topic only. As the event was over some time back, *past tense* is used throughout.

Note: In your academic life either at school or college, you get many opportunities to write reports on your School Day, Sports Day, Independence Day, Freshers Day etc. Sometimes you take part in an educational tour and on your return, you may be asked by the teacher to write a report on the tour. Or you might have taken part in a scout camp and you write a report at the end. Find here an example.

Example
Read here a report by the leader who took part in the Special Millennium Jamboree, as one of the scouts and guides:

Special Millennium Jamboree was held at Park View, Colombo, in Sri Lanka. Five guides and five scouts escorted by Mr Sukumaran of Kendriya Vidyalaya, Tirumalgiri, left Hyderabad for Colombo via Chennai.

In Chennai, we were joined by some more scouts and guides from Tiruvanantapuram, Bangalore and Mysore. Together we were 40 scouts and guides from South India, accompanied by four scout masters and the joint commissioner of Kendriya Vidyalaya Sanghatan. We collected our visas and left for Colombo after an hour's flying from Chennai. From Colombo we travelled by bus to the place where the camp was held. Our Jamboree site was on a hilltop and in the midst of a thick forest. A separate building was allotted for overseas scouts and guides. We took part in various activities of the Jamboree like cultural activities and march past. We also participated in adventure activities like shooting, commando crossing, tunnel crossing, rope clubbing and horse riding, elephant riding, cart driving, three wheeler driving, cycle repairing and ladder crossing.

In Colombo we were joined by contingents from Hong Kong, Malaysia and Sri Lanka. On the last day, we with the other contingents from different parts of the world went on a tour to places, like Kandy, Galle, Anuradapura and Kallutara and other places where we could experience the Sri Lankan culture and get a feel of it. We visited a famous temple where the Sri Lankans worship, a relic of the tooth of the Buddha. The entire contingent also paraded.

Our Jamboree came to an end after celebrating thinking day in memory of the birth anniversaries of the scout founders, Lord and Lady Baden Powel. After reaching India, we stayed a few hours at Chennai and the next morning we were in Hyderabad. I thank our teachers, scout master and above all god for this wonderful opportunity.

[Adapted from: 'Millennium Jamboree' by Srinivas, Std X, 'Quest', *The Hindu*, July14, 2001.]

Discussion:

In the above example, you might have observed the writer gave the essential particulars connected with the Special Millennium Jamboree only, in a sequential order. The writer mentioned the total number of scouts and guides of their school and others who joined them later. Thus, the necessary details from the starting point to the reaching point were given. Next, the writer gave the account of activities held at jamboree without letting out his/her feelings or excitement. As a whole, it is a good example of a work report/ report of an event.

EXERCISES

1. **Read the following report on water wastage in the city and break it down into**
   a) Terms of reference b) Proceedings c) Findings, d) Conclusions and e) Recommendations as in the normal business report, based on a survey:

The chief engineer of Hyderabad Metropolitan Water Supply and Sewerage Board (HMWSSB), submits a report, based on a survey, to the commissioner of Hyderabad Municipal Corporation, on approximate water wastage per day (MLD), by the people of Hyderabad, before the board meets on Oct15, 2001. The coordinator of the 12 committees appointed by the HMSSWB distributed a questionnaire to the citizens (about 12,000) and interviewed randomly some senior citizens, youth and experts on urban water management and other officers connected with the water supply. The coordinator and the members of the committees concluded that a huge amount of water, about 60% often goes into the drains. The inadequate supply of water by the corporation did not bring any change in the habits of the people or their attitude. The committee found that 60% MLD of the total water supplied, is wasted on whole by the citizens. 80% MLD of the wastage occurs at homes, as the people don't save water for use. If the water is stored at home, 40% MLD water can be saved. 53% MLD of water is wasted as tap or shower kept open during their bath. 75% MLD water can be saved if people keep the tap or shower closed during their bath and use when required. Similarly 30% MLD is wasted while people brush or shave and 90% MDL can be saved during such activities. While washing clothes and washing vessels and other cleaning works another 60% MLD is wasted.

[MLD – milli litres per day]

The table below gives more details:

Domestic Use	Water Used	Can be Saved
Shower bathing	2.49 MLD	39.36 MLD
Flush tank toilet	14.58 MLD	7.29 MLD
Shaving	29.83 MLD	26.85 MLD
Brushing teeth	34.56 MLD	31.10 MLD
Rinsing clothes	40.50 MLD	30.48 MLD

[from: *The Times of India*, June, 2001]

The coordinator of the committee feels that the wastage of water by the citizens can be reduced to a large extent if certain measures can be taken. It recommends that the people should be educated through the electronic media, posters, and short films in cinema theatres. As a part of it, a separate cell has to be established to monitor and supervise the use of water without wastage. The cell should have separate and exclusive staff to attend to repairs of all kinds including immediate and periodic repairs. A set of phones to be set up for getting information, on line, about wastage of water and urgent repairs. Water meters should be established. Periodic meetings should be organised between officials and representatives of water users. People should be educated through local TV channels, filmstrips, and other electronic media about different ways of saving water and there by awareness should be created about the value of water. There should be an officer of a chief engineer's rank who should be made responsible to control water wastage and attending to repairs.

2. **Read the report carefully and write the conclusions based on the findings and the information given in the tables.**
Title: A market survey on consumer preferences of small cars.
Terms of Reference: The Andhra Pradesh Regional Manager (Sales) is requested by the Marketing Manager (country), Maruti Udyog Limited to make a survey to find out the consumer preferences of various small cars along with the features that the

consumers look for while making a decision to purchase. The Report should be submitted before the next Board Meeting to be held on 23rd September, 2001.

Abstract: (of the Report) According to the survey, Daewoo Matiz is the most preferred car followed by Maruti (800 and Zen), Hyundai Santro, Tata Indica and Fiat Uno, in that order. The survey also found that looks (style) and comfort are the most sought after features while making a purchase decision.

Proceedings: The survey was conducted by asking the respondents to fill-up questionnaires. The findings of the survey based on the questionnaires and direct interviews with customers are as follows —-

Customers' preference to various cars

Cars	No of people
Maruti (800 and Zen)	25
Daewoo Matiz	35
Hyundai Santro	20
Fiat Uno	5
Tata Indica	15
Total Respondents	100

Customers' preference for different features

Features looked for	No. of People
Speed	30
Mileage	25
Pick-up	30
Interiors (Comfort)	40
Looks (Style)	50

Customers' preference for different features in cars

Features	Maruti	Daewoo	Hyundai	Fiat	Indica
Speed	6	7	6	5	5
Mileage	7	8	6	7	6
Pick-up	6	7	7	6	6
Interiors	5	6	5	5	6
Looks	6	7	5	4	5
Total Rating	30	35	29	27	28

Conclusions: ————————————————————
———————————————————————— [Write it]

Recommendations: The survey and findings suggest that the company should make the interiors more attractive and comfortable. The company should also think of introducing new models of Maruti 800 and Maruti Zen with higher engine capacity, with a view to increase the mileage. Looks wise also it can be more elegant and attractive to lure the customers.

3. *Here is a recommendation report (based on a survey). Read it carefully and complete it by writing terms of reference to the report.*

[Ms Uma Paudwal, the class teacher of XII asked a group leader of the same class to make a survey of the study habits of students aged between 14 to 16 years and submit a report, without recommendations, before Nov 3rd, 2001, as a part of children's day project]

Title: A report on the study habits of students aged between 14 to 16 years in our school and two neighbouring schools.

Terms of Reference: ————————————————
————————————————————————————
————————————————————————————

[Write it]

Proceedings: Rama Mathews and the members of her team made a survey of the study habits of the students in the age group of 14 to 16 years, to submit it, to the class teacher as part of term Project. The group leader, Ms Mathews, with the help of 4 more students of her class, prepared a questionnaire and distributed it to the students of her school who are between the age of 14 to 16 and also to the students of the same age who are in 2 neighbouring schools. Besides the answers she got from the questionnaire, she interviewed randomly some 223 students.

The results of the survey are as follows:
1. 90% of the students study seriously just one day before the unit test or term examinations or 1 week before the annual or final examinations. Rest of the time they utilise for home assignments.
2. 80% of the students prefer to study from 8.00 to 9.00 p.m.
3. 20% of the students prefer to study early in the morning from 5.00 to 7.00 a.m.
4. 10% of the students make a serious study every Sunday and utilise the time for things other than home assignment.
5. 70% of the girls study for more number of hours than the boys of their age.
6. 90% of the students in the school and others in the neighbouring schools too don't like to study between 9.00 to 10.00 p.m. as they have interesting programmes like Kaun Banega Crorepati (KBC) and India Quiz or other interesting programmes.
7. 70% of the girls study both at night, 8.00 to 9.00 p.m. and again early in the morning. They too prefer to watch T.V. from 9.00 to 10.00 p.m. for interesting programmes of their choice.
8. The reasons when investigated why many don't prefer to study at night between 9.00 to 10.00 p.m. is to watch their interesting programmes like KBC and cartoon films.

Conclusions
i) Majority of students aged between 14-16 don't study seriously every day because of the heavy home assignments, the temptation for TV to watch their interesting programme, KBC

or other programmes and physical tiresomeness caused by school activities, the whole day.

ii) Ninety per cent of students study before examinations only.

iii) A big majority of the students prefer to study only after 10.00 p.m. because it will be very calm and by then they finish routine class work and favourite programmes in the T.V.

iv) A good majority of girls prefer to study both after 10 p.m. and early in the morning also.

Recommendations: Not required.

4. *Read the following report (work report). Ms Komal Anand, director general, gave a report to the press after the Archaeological Survey of India (ASI) excavated the relics of Buddha. But the four paragraphs (a, b, c, d) of the report are not in the right order. Rewrite the report in the right order based on the examples.*

   a. Ms Anand, who is on a two-day visit to Jammu, told reporters on Thursday the relics of charred bones and ashes were found in a gold casket at the site on April 22, 2001.

   b. Stating that the relics belonged to Lord Buddha as the same have been discovered in seven other major stupas in the country and abroad by ASI, she said these would, however, be sent for DNA testing for confirmation.

   c. The golden casket was found in a copper reliquary which contained a silver casket, golden and silver leaves, beads of pearls, coral, carnelian and amethyst and three copper coins, she said.

   d. Buddha relics dating back to first century BC have been excavated by the Archaeological Survey of India (ASI) from the bank of river Chenab at Ambaran, about 29 km from here (Jammu), recently, according to the ASI Director General, Ms Komal Anand.

3.4 Reporting of Experiments (Laboratory Experiments)

The report of an experiment differs from a newspaper report in its format and general tone. The former is more precise and specific than the latter. Any report of an experiment is meant for a defined or specific reader unlike the other which is for a general reader. Similarly, the purpose of a Science report is for either learning or giving information as clearly as possible and briefly too. In the place of title, place and date, which you find in a newspaper report, you find other subtitles in a science report (Experiment) such as —

a) Aim
b) Apparatus/ Materials used
c) Theory (or principle)
d) Procedure/Method
e) Results (or observation)
f) Conclusions

In some experiments, if there is a large collection of data there may be an appendix and the results may be given in a tabular form. Before you write the report think of ———

Who is the reporter?
Who is s/he reporting to?
What is the purpose?
How is the report organised?

Example

Aim: To find out the melting point of wax

Apparatus: A beaker, thermometer, solid wax, Bunsen burner, and a stand

Theory: Substances exist in three states – solid, liquid and gaseous. They can be converted from one state to another by heating or cooling.

Procedure: Solid wax is taken in a beaker and a thermometer was arranged in a beaker with the help of a stand to hold it. The thermometer is kept in such a way that its bulb should be kept in contact with the wax. The solid wax in the beaker is heated with Bunsen burner. Every half minute the reading of the thermometer is noted. Initially, when the temperature is raised to a particular high point, the wax is seen melting. On further heating, temperature remained constant and the whole of solid wax is completely converted into a liquid state.

Observations: Solid wax melts at a constant temperature.
Conclusions: Wax melts into a liquid state from a solid state at a constant temperature.

Discussion

Here the reporter is a student of science who writes to others who know science (defined audience) and the purpose is for learning and to inform. The experiment is reported in the conventional format – aim, theory, apparatus etc. The I paragraph gives you the *aim* of the experiment. It is to find out the melting point of wax. The II paragraph gives you the *theory* which is nothing but preliminary or supporting information on which the experiment is based. The III paragraph deals with the list of *apparatus* such as beaker and thermometer etc. Sometimes you describe the apparatus if it is a complicated apparatus. The IV paragraph is the most important part of an experiment i.e., *procedure*. It deals with how actually the experiment is conducted step by step. The V and VI deal with the *observation* and *conclusion* respectively. At the end of the experiment, you note the observations. Based on the observations, you write your conclusions.

Example 2

Read another report of an experiment:

Aim: To determine that some amount of energy is generated from the oxidation of food materials in the form of heat.

Theory: Oxygen is an important factor in the control of respiration.

Apparatus / ingredients used: Two beakers, seeds, and thermos flask

Procedure: One day before the experiment, two beakers with seeds (like beans or peas) are taken. To one of the beakers water is added and the seeds are allowed to soak for the whole night. Dry seeds are kept in another beaker. Next morning, two thermos flasks, with a wide mouth, which can be closed with a tight fitting cork, are taken. The germinated seeds are transferred into one of the flasks and the dry fruits into the other flask. A hole is made in the cork of the flasks and the thermometers are inserted into these two flasks in such way that the bulb of the thermometer touches the seeds.

Temperatures are recorded every two or three hour intervals for about 24 hrs.

Observation: It is observed that the temperature in the flask with germinating seeds is higher than the temperature in the flasks with dry seeds.

Conclusion: Heat is liberated from the germinating seeds.

Discussion:

Here also, as in the previous experiment, the student is the reporter who is reporting to the defined audience and the purpose is learning and to inform. Now observe the *passive voice verbs* in every sentence, such as – *are taken, are kept, is added* etc. In a textbook, the writer instructs you 'take two beakers, add water, put a thermometer' etc (active voice). But when you write it in the form of a report in the record notebook, you have to follow a certain format such as aim, theory, apparatus, procedure etc and the verbs should be in passive voice, generally. So the format of a science report is different from a newspaper report, in many ways. Thus, the two experiments given above will tell you how to write an experiment with a particular format.

Exercises

1. *Here is an incomplete report. It has aim, apparatus/ ingredients, theory, procedure and results/observation but not conclusion. Read the Report and complete it by writing the conclusion in one or two lines.*

Aim: To remove impurities from water and make it fit for drinking purposes.

Apparatus/Ingredients/ Things: Sedimentation tank*, alum, layers of sand, chlorine

Theory: The water we use for drinking purposes must be clean and safe. It must be free from bacterial impurities and some of dissolved salts as well.

Procedure: Water from the source (river, tank or lake) is pumped through pipes into sedimentation tank. To this tank alum is added

---

* A Tank filled with layers of sand to let the water flow on it so that the gravel, mud or the other impurities will be settled on it and water be purified.

to quicken the sedimentation of suspended impurities. This water is then sent into a filter tank where it passes through a thick layer of fine sand. Here insoluble particles get settled on the layer of sand. Then the water is treated with chlorine which kills the disease causing germs. This purified and disinfected water is supplied to our homes as drinking water.

Observation: This purified water is clean, colourless and when examined under a microscope, is free from germs.

Conclusion: ——————————————————————
(Write it)

2. **Given below are the instructions for a science experiment. Read it carefully. Prepare a report as the one you read above.**
Determination of melting point of ice and boiling point of water: Take some pure ice pieces in a glass beaker and measure the temperature with a Celsius thermometer. Let the temperature be 100°c. Heat the beaker with the Bunsen burner and note down the temperatures at intervals of half minute. The temperature rises up to 0°c when the ice starts melting and then remains constant until all the ice melts into water. If the heating is continued further the temperature rises until 1000°c when the water starts boiling. Until all the water boils and evaporates there will not be any change in temperature. This constant temperature is called its boiling point.

3. **Write a mock report on how to prepare 'Instant Rava Dosa' (pan cake), based on the instructions given below:**
To one measure of this mix (500g) of the packet, add two measures (1.25 ltrs) of water. Stir to a smooth batter and keep aside for 5 minutes. Heat 'dosa tava' and smear it well with oil. Spread one cup (60ml) of batter on tava. Fry one side on low flame. Drop a spoonful of ghee if required. Rub the *tava* lightly with damp cloth for surface cooling and repeat the preparation process. You can add chopped green coriander leaves, green chilli and finely chopped onions to the batter for better taste. From this 500g pack, you can prepare 25 rava dosas of normal size, each weighing about 30-35g.

Alternately, batter can be prepared in the same way using ½ measure of curd/yoghurt and 1and1/2 measures of water instead of 2 measures of water.

3.5 Reporting of Meetings (Minutes of a Meeting)

Our young learners or the senior students at the college or university, might have or will have the experience of holding sports, cultural and other organisational meetings. Later also, when they take up a job, business or become the members of an association, social organization or a club, they will have the experience of holding meetings and write minutes of a meeting. When they hold meetings of any sort they transact business and take certain resolutions. These resolutions will be recorded at the end of the meeting and they will be read out in the next meeting. They are called *Minutes of a Report.*

What are Minutes?

Minutes are a brief authentic or legal record of decisions or resolutions taken at a committee, board or other formal meetings. It attempts to record on paper what went on at a meeting and especially to know what was decided or transacted by the members.

Main Components of Minutes:

- Date, time and place of the meeting.
- Names of the chairperson/president and secretary.
- Names of those present at the meeting including special invitees, if any.
- Letters by the members expressing regret for their absence, if any.
- List of resolutions made by the members one by one in an order.

Why Minutes?

- To help the members of the committee to know what happened in the previous meeting.
- To give information to the members who are absent.
- To facilitate the committee to confirm the resolutions taken in the meeting on paper by the members present or absent.
- To circulate the copy of minutes among the members.
- To keep the record for future reference.

Kinds of Minutes—
a) Informal notes, usually attached to and commenting on files of papers much like memoranda
b) Brief, formal record of decisions taken at a committee, board or other formal meetings.
c) Descriptive report of the proceedings at a meeting summarising the discussion and recording the decisions taken.
But this unit deals with minutes, which are most commonly used variety that is the second variety (b). These kinds of minutes contains a list of decisions taken at a committee, board or other formal meetings. And the decisions are recorded briefly and clearly.

Note: Any kind of minutes stated above should be preceded by an agenda.

Example
Study the following minutes of a meeting:

College Union Sports Club
Meeting to be held in the Auditorium Annexe
On Monday, at 5.00 p.m.
August 20th, 2001.

Agenda of the Meeting
1. Apologies for absence
2. Approval of the Minutes of the last meeting
3. Matters arising from the last Minutes
4. Finalising the programme for the coming Sports Day
5. Any other business
6. Date of the next meeting

Minutes of the Meeting
The executive committee of the College Union Sports Club, held the meeting on August 20, 2001, (Monday), at 5.00 p.m. in the auditorium annexe.

Members present:
1. Dr. Rishikesh Tiwari — (Dean Student Counseling) – Special Invitee

2. Mr Naleenaksha   III B Sc (President)
3. Ms Malati   II B Com (Ladies Secretary)
4. Mr Rakesh Das.   II B Sc (Sports Secretary)
5. Ms Neelima Hattangadi   II B A (Secretary, Arts Students)

Letters, from the following members expressing regret for their inability to attend, were read out.

a. A K Sreenivas III B.Sc
b. Ms Rekha II B.A.

  i) The minutes of the last meeting held on March 4, 2001 were read out by Mr Rakesh Das, the sports secretary, and were confirmed and signed.

  ii) The members resolved the following —
    a. To request the principal to hold Sports Day in the last week of January, to avoid distraction to the students before their examinations.
    b. To felicitate Mr P Gopi Chand, winner of All England Badminton Championship, 2001, on the coming Sports Day to be held.
    c. To add one more event i.e., Chess tournament from this year onwards, in the list of competitions to be held on Sports Day
    d. To hold the next meeting of the Sports Club on January 30, 2002.

  iii) The secretary proposed a vote of thanks and the meeting dissolved at 6.30 p.m.

Discussion

You might have observed in the above minutes that the agenda is followed by the minutes. The agenda is nothing but a programme sheet which informs the members what is going to be discussed in the meeting. The members of the committee should know beforehand what is going to be discussed in the meetings. Hence the agenda precedes the minutes. It is something like a brief which you prepare for a business report (based on a survey). Similarly, the minutes also have a clear procedure which you might have observed as above. The minutes of a meeting is a record, containing a title which contains the name of the committee, time, date, and place of the meeting held. Then the members present are listed with their signatures. The minutes of the previous meeting are read out. Then follows the list of resolutions or recommendations one after another. At the end, the date of the next meeting is stated. Thus, every incident that takes place in the meeting is recorded briefly, clearly and chronologically. As minutes are written after the meeting was held, *past tense* is used and the language should be simple and free from ambiguity.

Exercises
1. *The following is the agenda of the executive committee of the college Union with the student President Mr Suresh Yadav in the chair. At the end of the agenda, see the task. You can add any other necessary details like place, name of the college etc of your own.*

Agenda:
a) Letters of apology from the members who are absent
b) Approval of the minutes of the last meeting
c) Matters arising from the last minutes
d) Elections to elect new president and secretary and other representatives
e) To finalise the programme for Freshers' day
f) To conduct literacy camps from Sept to Nov 2002
g) Any other business
h) Date of next meeting

Task:
You form into a group of 5 or 6 and each member should enact the role of one of the members of the college union. Like that other groups also can be formed. Discuss each item of the agenda and then prepare the minutes of the meeting.

2. *You are the secretary of the Cultural Association of A V College of Arts and Science, Lucknow. Write the minutes of the meeting and prepare an agenda also. You can use the following notes:*

The Cultural Association met on 26th Dec, at 4.30 p.m. in the seminar hall of the college. Subject: Meeting of the executive Body of the Cultural association. Members present: Dr. V K Gupta, President, Mr Naresh Agarwal, Secretary, members: 1.———— 2.————.3. ———————— 4. —————. 5. —————. Letters of apology from Mr. Krishna Kanth, III BA, and Aneesha Saxena, III B Sc. The minutes of the previous meeting held on Sep 3rd, 2001, was read out by the secretary. The committee resolved to take part in the north zone cultural inter-university competitions to be held in Jan 2002. Resolved to send 1 team for enacting Hindi drama and another one for a group dance and two teams, each four, for group songs and fancy dress. A resolution is made to request the principal to grant Rs. 8000/ to buy certain music instruments and dresses etc. Next meeting will be held in March, 2002.

*****

IV

Scholarly Writing

When the young learners complete their graduation or post graduation (masters), they are exposed to higher or advanced writing like term papers, dissertation or doctoral thesis which are commonly termed as *Scholarly Writing*. For writing them, they need another set of writing skills which are entirely different from the previous examination i.e., oriented and structured writings which they use at under or postgraduation levels. When they write the dissertation, research or term papers or doctoral thesis, they are free from the shackles of a set syllabus, stereotyped questions, an outline, word limit or other kinds of closed guidance. In other words, at higher levels, they are exposed to a more open, self-guided, reference or investigation oriented, formal advanced writing. Generally, the advanced students need to write and submit anyone of them for fulfilling the formalities to get certain higher degrees like postgraduation or research degree. Moreover, all these writings make the learners to be skilled in using various reference materials like encyclopaedias, research abstracts, periodicals, various kinds of bibliographies, subject dictionaries, Companions and other reference materials. Based on the *primary sources*[*] and reference materials, they write the dissertation/ term papers etc., following certain norms and regulations and fulfil the requirements to get the degree. Finally, these skills of reference and writing lead her/him to evolve their own style and be a scholar in due course and equip them to do further research and writing.

---

[*] See Glossary

Many facilities have come into use for scholars to do research and the very scenario of research has been changed for the last 10 years or so in India and 15 years abroad. Due to the widespread use of personal computers (PC), the advancements in IT and other technologies, interconnection of libraries, creation of innumerable websites and online databases, a scholar can get ample information, do reference work and copy or read anything on the globe, in the shortest possible time. One need not go from one library to another and travel. Even in a library also, after the introduction of online (computerisation of) catalogues, one need not physically go through the cards standing before the catalogue desks. All these facilities motivate a prospective scholar and reduce her/his time in doing reference. But the rest of the work should be done personally. On the writing front also, the scholar can reduce a lot of time by using a PC or laptop/notebook. The use of computers for writing has brought certain advantages like inserting tables, graphs, charts (MS Excel), autoshapes and clipart pictures etc. The set of operations in MS Word, like the spell check, correction of language use, punctuation, auto correct and other facilities in the computer, are of great support to the scholar to edit the text. But a machine may crash at any time and has its own limitations. Keeping aside the limitations, no body can deny the fact that the extensive use of PCs has reduced the time for reference work, writing and editing, to a great extent and improved the quality of research.

This chapter aims to give some guidelines for the prospective scholars who are involved in writing dissertation, term papers, research paper and doctoral thesis. It also tries to help the scholars, at the initial level, with various reference materials and advanced writing skills. In fact, no single chapter or book can satisfy the scholar to know everything, and one can be proficient in the skills by complete involvement only. The best way of learning is doing and it should be done consistently. The same is the case with scholarly writing.

In fact, getting practice in scholarly writing and attaining a degree in higher education or Ph D degree is not an end in itself but a beginning only. One cannot expect becoming a scholar instantly with the degree. The Ph D degree boosts scholars' self-confidence to use her/his skills for advanced writing. Further, the degree makes her/him more productive and motivates them to pursue further research and write articles, papers and books, besides being qualified for suitable job opportunities.

Dissertation, Term Papers, Research Paper and Doctoral Thesis:

As stated already, dissertation, term papers etc., are part of scholarly writing which involve a lot of reference and advanced writing skills. Generally, they are written, as a part of college activity to fulfill the requirements of getting MA/MSc and other postgraduate degrees. Whereas an M Phil degree requires both term papers and thesis. In many universities in India, a dissertation is submitted to fulfil the requirements of a postgraduate degree and a thesis is submitted to get a Ph D degree. But in some countries, these two terms are used interchangeably and considered synonyms. The basic skills of reference and writing are common in all these writings, though there are certain differences.

There are many differences between one kind of scholarly writing and the other. Among them, a doctoral thesis stands apart and is different from all the rest of them in many ways. Very rarely, we find words like a 'Masters' 'Thesis' and 'doctoral dissertation' in India. Whereas, in the U.S, the term, doctoral dissertation is used instead of Ph D Thesis. In this chapter, the writer uses the term, dissertation for the postgraduation degree and thesis for the Ph. D. In fact, a doctoral thesis is far superior and advanced, than all other kinds of writings like dissertation, term paper and research paper. A doctoral thesis is an independent work based on original research, guided by an expert and adjudged by institutional experts in the field and contributes to the advancement of knowledge on a particular subject. Further, reputed scholars in the field adjudicate the thesis. On successfully completing the research, a degree is conferred on the scholar after certain formalities like viva voce (interview), as per the regulations of the university. The one common factor among all of them, except the research paper, is getting a degree after due submission of dissertation or thesis.

A research paper is different from the other kinds of scholarly writings for the reason that it is not meant for getting a degree or to fulfil the requirements of a course. It is written either to publish it in a journal or to present it in a conference or both. At the same time, it shares the skills of reference, getting information or data, analysing and writing objectively.

4.1 Dissertation

As stated earlier, there is no common agreement in the use of the term, 'dissertation' among the colleges/universities. But in the Indian context, a dissertation is submitted to fulfil the requirements of getting a postgraduate degree. Unlike the doctoral thesis, it is not an original study and hence does not contribute to the advancement of knowledge. The scholar who prepares for writing a dissertation has to do a considerable amount of reference work and learn the skills of advanced writing. Generally, the topic will be given by the professor/supervisor/advisor concerned, unlike in the case of a doctoral thesis. Learners will be trained to probe, investigate a topic and collect information from various sources like bibliographies and journals etc. The one who submitted a dissertation and learnt the skills of scholarly writing will have an edge over others when s/he takes up doctoral studies later.

The scholar who is involved in writing the dissertation needs a lot of preparation with regard to reference work and getting information about rules and regulations of the institution/department. A number of formalities have to be fulfilled to submit her/his dissertation. These formalities differ from one university/institute to another and in the country or abroad

Note: High standards or originality is not expected from students of dissertation. It is mainly meant to give the learners practice in how to probe, investigate, analyse and conclude a given topic. It is something like an apprenticeship or training in doing reference work and expose the scholar to various reference materials and to scholarly writing.

Format:
Often, the format depends on the conventions of the university/college. What follows is a set of general practices usually followed

in any institute. There may be slight variations in the practices and conventions of submitting a dissertation, from university/college to the other.
  i. Cover page includes the topic of the dissertation, name of the student, the degree for which it is submitted, name of the supervisor/professor whose guidance taken, and name of the college/ university from which it is submitted and the year of submission..
  ii. The same text (matter) on the cover page is replicated and kept on the inner cover page.
  iii. Contents,
  iv. Preface and Acknowledgements
  v. Introduction, if necessary, and then
  vi. The text of the Dissertation in chapters.
  vii. Bibliography or Select Bibliography

Some guidelines:
1. Learners use A-4 size white paper and computer typed with margins 1 or 1 and ½ on four sides of the page.
2. Footnotes/endnotes, bibliography and citations are included where necessary.
3. At the end of the section or chapter, a list of references will be given as per the *MLA Handbook* (latest edition) regulations.
4. After a number of proof readings, you prepare the final draft and get it spiral bound with the cover page and title page printed according to the conventions of the college/university and get the number of copies duly signed by the supervisor and you.
5. The number of copies of the dissertation to be submitted varies from one university to another.

Language and Style:
  1. Any kind of scholarly writing should be fairly readable and simple. Never use ornate or pompous style.
  2. The language of any scholarly writing should be free from being verbose and clichés. You should neither give personal experience, opinions nor use personal pronouns or direct speech except in quotations.

3. The sentences should not be too involved or long and unwieldy.
4. Sweeping statements and exaggerated claims should be avoided.
5. Use quotations contextually and quote exactly with acknowledgements. You should acknowledge a quotation giving the reference particulars, in the footnotes/end notes, as per the norms given in *MLA handbook*. They should fit into the main running text by agreeing with subject and verb. If they do not fit in, omit certain words putting small dashes or dots.
6. If you don't acknowledge a quotation you will be charged with *plagiarism* which is a serious academic crime or a sort of piracy.
7. Assist your reader by signposting your argument by using appropriate linking words.
8. Avoid, first and second person pronouns; repetitions, excessive wordiness, too many quotations, overused phrases and clichés.
9. No body will excuse the writer's spelling or grammatical mistakes and there is a set limit (5 or 6) even for the typographical mistakes. Follow consistently either British or American spelling. The computer spell check is helpful to some extent only and it is programmed to American spelling and usage. Better check the spell check done by the computer.
10. During the process of writing a research paper, doctoral thesis or any scholarly writing, you should evolve your own style which should look like a natural flow but not imposed from above. "A good style should show no sign of effort. What is written should seem a happy accident" ✦

Checklist:
i. Cover Page, ii. Inner Cover. iii Preface, and Acknowledgements together in one page or separately, some topics may need

---

✦ Somerset Maugham

introduction also, iv. Contents, v. Text of the Dissertation, chapter by chapter, and vi. Conclusions. vii. Bibliography

Note: When you give references, footnotes or bibliography you have to follow the models given in *MLA Handbook*, the latest edition.

4.2 Term Papers

Students mainly at the postgraduate level or M Phil are required to write term papers. Rarely, we find that the students at the undergraduate level too are asked to submit term papers. Generally, Term papers, like the dissertation, are a part of the college activity or the course to fulfil the formalities to get the degree (Postgraduate), besides the written examinations. And students have to submit certain minimum number of papers to complete the course. Term papers often deal with a topic involving some problem, investigation, or an expository topic, connected with their course. Very often, the topic will be suggested by the professor concerned, unlike at the Ph D level.

It is true as Kaplan and Shaw say: 'Writing a Term Paper is an introductory exercise intended to teach students about scholarly writing'[*]. It is something like initiating the learner into the art of scholarly writing and letting her/him to enjoy the fruits of it. The expertise, gained at this level, will be a great asset when s/he takes up research or Ph D, later. While writing term papers, s/he is exposed to various reference sources like encyclopaedias, bibliographies, and subject journals etc., and learn doing reference. Besides, they will be skilled in preparing bibliography cards and note cards and others on a mini scale. Another benefit of writing term papers is that they learn the art of writing objectively and impersonally based on facts and it is the essential quality of scholarly writing. The main difference between the term papers and the doctoral study is in its gamut, scope, depth, and intensity and above all, in originality.

---

[*] Robert B. Kaplan, and Peter A. Shaw. *Exploring Academic Discourse,* London: Newbury House Publication Inc, 1983, Appendix-2

This kind of writing trains the learners to write objectively and without any bias, and it gives practice in summarising their observations, giving references where needed. To be brief, a term paper is an opportunity and provides training in the basics of scholarly writing, as stated already. Of all, it whets the interest in the chosen field, at least some learners may take up research later. The text of the paper like other writings is divided into three main bodies — introduction, main body, conclusion.

Format:
Often, the format depends on the conventions of the university/ college. What follows is a set of general practices. Sometimes they may vary from one institute/university to another.
i. Cover page which includes the topic of the term paper, name of the student, name of the course to which it is submitted, name of the supervisor/professor whose guidance taken, and name of the college/ university, where it is submitted, ii. Title of the term paper, iii. Contents, iv. Preface and Acknowledgements and Introduction, if necessary and then text of the paper chapterwise.

Some guidelines:
Refer to the section in dissertation.

Language and Style:
Refer to the section in dissertation.

Checklist:
Refer to the section in dissertation.

4.3 Research Paper

Research is meant to fill in certain gaps in a particular field or knowledge in general. It is a critical, analytical, investigative, and disciplined study to find a solution for a problem or explore an unexplored area. The study of an investigation into a topic may include exploration, experiments, analysis, interviews, tour, field study, reading old records, and synthesis etc. But all papers may not include all these. Eventually, the research will lead to certain findings and conclusions based on the study. Like thesis writing (Ph. D), a research paper is also based on original study and the difference is that no degree is awarded for it. Though not a degree, a research paper has its own merits which you will know in the following pages. The merits of learning how to write a research paper are not limited to the academic field alone. It helps you in your professional career also when you write certain reports based on secondary research wherein you consult sources of information about a particular subject. It is a work done on a mini scale and mono-dimensional with a limited range and scope. In some universities the students are asked to publish a minimum number of research papers before they get a doctoral degree. Doing reference work by studying resource materials like encyclopaedias, bibliographies, and subject journals etc., and collect information, on a chosen topic, will be the same as that of thesis writing. The difference between them is the range and depth of study. Preparing bibliography and note cards are the same as with other scholarly writing.

    A research paper can be *descriptive, interpretative (interpretive), exploratory or experimental.* Others classify research into *exploratory, testing-out and problem solving.* Whatever the classification, one should find out her/his own way of presenting the arguments based on the nature of the topic. Phillips and Pugh have aptly said "Doing research is a craft skill, which is why the basic educational process that takes place is that of learning by doing"* . So unless you take up research, you cannot get the skills. Whatever one takes up either descriptive or interpretive kind, the basic format or structure will be the same—introduction, main body and conclusion and this is common with the other scholarly writings.

    A research paper begins with a *preliminary hypothesis* and ends with a confirmation, rejection or modification. This is something like a thesis or thesis statement which serves as a starting point. Or one may call it a preliminary thesis also. The statement of preliminary hypothesis rouses interest in the readers who specialise

---

* Estelle M. Phillips and D. S. Pugh *How to get a Ph. D,* Milton Keynes: Philadelphia, Open University Press, 1987. (P. 47)

in that field and it helps the researcher to guide her/him like the map without being distracted. It will be like a brief summary in the beginning itself, giving focus, the different aspects of the topic and the strategy, the researcher follows.

After the preliminary hypothesis, it is better to give a summary of the research done in the past by the previous researchers on the topic or related topic. In other words, it is nothing but a *survey* of the previous study and their findings on the topic.

The main body of the paper deals with the *central thesis* which contains the different stages of investigation, data, arguments, analysis of the data upon which the conclusions are based. The paper from the beginning to the end should be well argued and organised with a sequence of arguments and evidence based on facts. A good research paper should evolve in a natural graded way from the preliminary thesis to central thesis and to the conclusion.

The last section of the paper deals with conclusions arrived from the study and investigation or analysis. Or in a way conclusions are the summary of your research findings and arguments stated in the body.

Purpose:
Generally, research papers are prepared for a personal use like publishing it in a subject journal or presenting it in a conference or both. In some universities and institutions, the faculty has to present a minimum number of research papers as credits to get promotions. More than anything else, a scholar who has published a number of research papers will definitely have an edge over others in getting scholarly acumen.

Some guidelines:
1. Needs number of drafts: The more you revise the better for you. Any paper improves after many revisions and redrafting. Avoid repetitive statements.
2. Spell check: It is better not to depend on the computer spell check as it goes with American usage, spelling and word compounds. Nothing should be taken for granted in any research.

3. Tables/Charts: Some research papers need tables or charts. It takes less time for those who use a PC to insert tables, charts or graphics.
4. Research paper must be double-spaced including footnotes and the list of works cited. Leave margins of one inch at the top and bottom and on both sides of the text.
5. It has all notes as endnotes without choice, unless you are instructed otherwise.

Note: Follow the latest edition of the *MLA Handbook* for the norms to write the references and footnotes etc. They are common with any kind of scholarly writing.

Language and Style:
Refer to the section in dissertation

To sum up: observe the chart

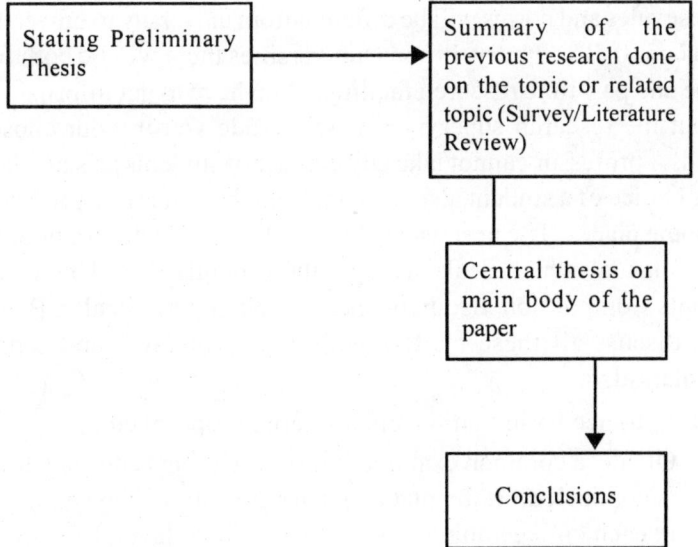

4.4 Thesis

A Thesis has a wider scope than any other scholarly writing in depth and range. As already stated, it is an independent work based on original research and contributes to the knowledge in a particular field. The preparation connected with the doctoral thesis is generally of two kinds——

4.4.1 Preparation

After you decide to do research you have to do a lot of preparation which includes——

a. Institutional Rules b. Selecting a Topic

a. *Institutional Rules*

At the outset, you have to be acquainted with the institutional rules and facilities available in the university you selected. You get to know the terms and regulations regarding registration, whether there is an entrance examination to write and other procedures. These rules and norms will be different from university to university and country to country. In some universities there will be both full time and part time research facilities. You have to get information about the research supervisors* who guide you in your chosen field. A professor cannot take any number of students as s/he likes. The choice of a student also may not be in the hands of a professor in some places. The best way to know all these is getting a booklet or a manual which deals with all these regulations. University Grants Commission also publishes a booklet periodically. Better you discuss all these matters with your professors and senior scholars also.

> **i.** Entrance Examination and Research Proposal etc.
>
> Of late, a common examination at the national and state level is conducted, in the place of separate entrance examination in each college/university. At the National level, UGC NET examination and at the state level SLET are conducted for allowing the students to qualify them to register for the Ph D. If the scholars are successful in these examinations they will have a double advantage like qualifying themselves for registering for the Ph D and getting eligibility to apply for a

faculty position in a college/university, depending upon the percentage of marks. Those who get a higher rank will get scholarship (JRF) also. As a result, the successful students of NET or SLET can directly register for the Ph D.

 ii. Further, find out whether you have to submit the *research proposal, synopsis* or any other in that place and the time given to do that.
 iii. Study all the rules and regulations in the booklet connected with fees for registration and rules connected with submission etc., and the time allowed to submit the thesis, and the extension period if necessary.
 iv. If you are not a UGC scholar or sponsored candidate, find out whether the university offers any scholarship or permits part time jobs on the campus or elsewhere.

b. *Selecting a Topic:*

Selecting a topic for doctoral thesis is the most crucial part and one should do a lot of reading and be patient and cautious. Selecting a good feasible topic is like half the work done. Generally, in the case of term papers and dissertations etc., the topic will be suggested by the professor concerned. But for a doctoral thesis the prospective scholar has to do a lot of probing by reading reference books, old theses, online search and discussing with professors in the field. *Even if you take six months time to select a topic it does not matter*[*]. But don't expect that somebody will suggest you a topic. In a few places, it is commonly observed that a professor would suggest a topic and the scholar simply accepts it. But the best way is that the scholar herself/ himself should do some probing by studying a number of journals, recent articles, research abstracts/dissertation abstracts, and old research work done on the topic/subject or writer and then should come out with a topic. Some scholars may find a topic at the postgraduation level while writing dissertation or term papers.

One should be cautious, in selecting a topic *and never be swept away by some fancy topic or favourite writer or any momentary*

---
[*] Emphasis added.

attraction. If you want to be practical, select a topic which is something workable, feasible and viable to carry on research in the stipulated time. Mere interest in a topic leads you nowhere. Your decision to take up a topic must depend mainly on the availability of the *primary sources*. Another factor which you should be careful is to ensure that the very topic was not done by another scholar, with the same title. In case, it has been done already, you may alter or modify the topic by taking another aspect of the topic, with the consultation of your supervisor.

To Sum up

Decide whether to do research.

Decide the field of interest, where to do (University/PG Centre), what stream—full-time or part-time research etc.

Interact with professors and discuss possible topics of your interest and have 3 or 4 topics on your mind.

Prepare for NET or SLET examination.

How to Select a Topic?

Thanks to the latest developments in technology. You can search for any topic, book/journal on the net in a short time. As a result, the scholars' time to search for a topic in a website reduces much of her/his time. There are many search engines like Google, Gurunet or Yahoo etc. All the libraries are interconnected with one another, through INFIBLINET, programme. In addition to the use of websites etc., many universities, in India too have computerised their libraries and the online catalogues can be searched on the computer which takes less time than manual search. After selecting the books, you go to the racks, get them and read. In some bookstores, you can get dictionaries or encyclopaedias in the electronic media like CDs. Use of copying machines also lessened much of the work of the scholars. Of late, there is an inter-library loan facility also. Besides, there are a number of websites of bookstores which you can surf and know the titles, publication details and contents of the book. And every reputed journal has a website. All these devices help the scholars to make a survey of various topics and select one in a reasonable time. It does not mean that you have to use only the electronic devices and Internet and select a topic. At one level or the other you have to do reference work offline also. The moot question is how far these facilities and technology are within the reach of the scholars in different parts of our country. Any way there is a lot of progress between what it was and now.

4.4.2 Reference Materials
a. General (for broader search):
- Various Encyclopaedias and Indexes
- Book Review Digest
- Bulletin of New York Public Library
- Dictionary of National Bibliography by Oxford
- The International Who's Who (EUROPA)
- Encyclopaedia of Indian Literature (Sahitya Academy)
- Guide to Indian Periodical Literature (Social Sciences and Humanities)
- Various Bibliographies on a particular topic/major International Events /Writers etc.
- Reader's Guide to Periodical Literature

b. Online Search: Search engines like Google, Gurunet and Yahoo are very famous for searching topics subjectwise like humanities, arts, sciences etc, which you can navigate through, till you get a specific field. Some search engines direct you to other links to find specific sites. Sometimes you would like to surf some famous bookstores like Barnes & Noble and Amazon where you can search for an author or book titles or other details. There are some online databases like INFOTRAC and Thomson Learning.

c. Materials to narrow the topic:
After referring to general source materials and selecting a broader field, narrow your field. You start referring to particular sources connected to your field. You may refer to—
- Subject Journals* some old and new ones

---
* Many reputed international and subject journals have exclusive websites, some are free and some are personal services which are available on payment.

- Dissertation Abstracts/Research Abstracts
- Articles written on your chosen topic/writer
- Handbooks, and others

d. Old Theses

After you have narrowed down the topic by referring to them select two or three topics temporarily and later one and then read old theses/dissertations written on the topic/field or similar topic. In this case, many universities have annual bulletins which may be useful. A directory of various Ph D theses awarded in the country also will be available. With the help of inter-library loan facility you may get it. You may find eventually a topic/field which is not much researched.

For example, you decide to do research in twentieth century Indian literature and a particular poet. Then you may select a relevant bibliography or encyclopaedia wherein the poet's works are referred to. You may find the works of the poet in the reference materials and critical books, and articles written on her/him. Next you may search whether there is a biography on her/him or letters written by the poet.

Note:
1. Some who had the experience of writing dissertation/term papers etc., already, will be familiar with areas of research and develop interest in a particular area and select a topic for the Ph D, then itself.
2. For all the reference work whether general or particular, you should have a time frame and use speed-reading techniques meant for reference. There is no point for being frustrated by seeing the size of the volumes and numbers.

4.4.3 Discussion with Professors or Experts in the Field

After selecting two or three topics discuss it with your research supervisor, professors, and experts in the field and then get your research supervisor's approval and later finalise a topic.

Survey (Literature Review)

Make a survey of the previous research done on the topic/field, with a view to find out what research was done by others in the field and what was left. In some universities, it is called *Literature Review*. It can be done by studying books, articles, old theses and others on the topic or related topic. In fact, any research is meant to fill in gaps in a branch of knowledge. Your survey on the topic will help you to take up the threads left by them. And later you can include the material in the introduction of your thesis.

To sum up:
Before the actual study begins, a lot of preparation is necessary, as revealed above.

Observe the chart——

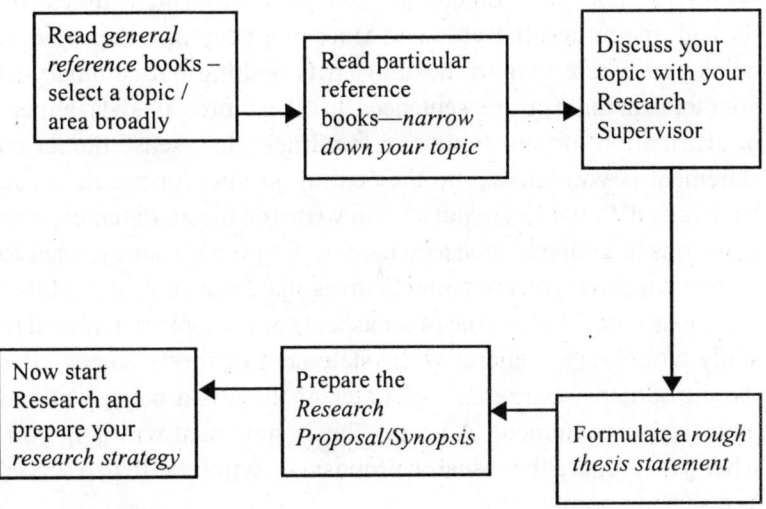

Check List:
- Whether all the primary sources on the topic/writer are available.
- Whether there are enough reference materials (secondary sources) on the selected topic.
- Whether you are confident that the topic is viable and workable within the stipulated time.

- Whether your research supervisor* or a professor who specialised the topic, approved your topic. Find out whether you are confident to strike a rapport with her/him and carry on the research.
- Have you surveyed the previous research done on the topic? Have you studied some old theses related to your selected topic?
- Avoid——
  Most recent, most sensitive or controversial topic.
  The topic on which no primary sources are available.
  Politically or religiously sensitive topic.
  The topics on which still research is going on.

4.4.4. Formulate a Rough Thesis Statement:

A *thesis statement* is something like a road map which guides you through the unfamiliar area and takes you deep into the topic. It helps you where you are heading. It is nothing but summary of your topic in three or four sentences. In other words, it is a statement or affirmation of your topic in a few lines. 'In a sense the thesis statement is your answer to the central question or problem you have raised'✢. If you are not able to write the thesis statement, put questions to yourself such as what you are going to study, what to investigate, how you are going to investigate and analyse the topic etc. Then state what are the other aspects of the topic you intend to study tentatively. Generally, the statement of thesis comes after the introductory paragraph(s). Later, if there is a need, you can modify your statement. A proper thesis statement will help you, when you prepare the research proposal or synopsis. It also serves as a starting point.

4.4.5. Research Proposal

In some universities a *Research Proposal* is called *approval sheet*. There is no commonly agreed format for the research proposal but

---

* Sometimes the field you selected for research and that of your Research Supervisor's may not be the same.

✢ Joseph. Gibaldi, *MLA Handbook for Writers of Research Papers (Sixth Edition)*, New Delhi: Affiliated East–West Press, 2004, P. 49-50.

if prepared with care and attention, it will serve as an *action plan* in fact, and guide you step by step like a map.

The proposal should give a clear idea of what you want to do and how you want to do. The reader or the committee who approves your proposal wants to know how your study fits into others' work on the topic. If your proposal does not clearly state your purpose and plan of study it is difficult for the committee to evaluate your proposal. It should reveal the exact topic and its importance stating that the topic has not been done by previous scholars. If the topic is done by others tell how your study contributes with a new aspect or dimension. You may give the statement of hypothesis also in the proposal. Better if you would mention the sources of information, your strategy to investigate the topic, your methodology, like questionnaire, interviews, data etc. By then, if you can visualise the whole topic, give an outline of the topic or list the contents. Or give subtitles which reflect the different aspects of the topic which you are going to deal with.

As stated earlier, if done properly, the proposal is nothing but your action plan. So you may estimate the possible time for each phase of your research and mention the approximate time you take for reference work, preparing cards, investigation, tours, interviews, preparing questionnaire and preparation of charts/tables, depending on the nature of the topic, and the possible time when you start preparing the first draft etc., based upon the total time a scholar is given. However, you can make any changes later when you progress in your study, though you have not mentioned them in your proposal.

Note: You need not wait or waste time waiting for the approval of your research proposal by the committee. You can continue your reference work and reading the primary sources, pending to the approval of your proposal.

Proposal includes—
- Full title
- Statement of hypothesis
- Methodology

- Approximate time schedules
- Expected results

Prepare the Rough Draft:
After getting a mental view of the whole thesis or a comprehensive plan and developed the topic to a large extent, write the first rough draft, chapterwise and with subtitles.

Revise your first draft
You may need to revise the whole thesis 3 or 4 times generally. As you revise, it develops mentally and it can be seen on the paper. As long as the thesis improves, revision after revision, there is no reason to be discouraged by the number of drafts and the time it takes. When you revise the draft you should follow certain conventions of the language, which follow shortly, used in thesis writing.

Abstract
After finalising your thesis, you have to prepare the abstract of your thesis, as per the conventions of the university. Nowadays it is included in the first few pages of the thesis, instead of a separate sheet. Many universities here and abroad follow the convention. The abstract conveys to the potential readers the essential information of your study, in the form of a summary. It tells the readers what you studied, how you studied, what you found out and what your conclusions and recommendations are, based on your analysis. You should put proper effort while preparing and finalising the abstract because it will be published in the 'dissertation abstracts' and becomes a public record. It will help the examiners to have a bird's eye view of your study and later the readers who use it as a reference in the beginning of their research. It is important that you should follow the word limit, as per the conventions of the university while preparing the abstract.

Conventions of the Language[*] :
  1. *Language*: The language of thesis writing should be objective and impersonal.

---
[*] Some of the points are repeated in connection with Dissertation.

2. It should have a coherent, logical development of arguments from the beginning to the end to enable smooth reading. One should follow the conventions of the written language.
3. Avoid an ornate or pompous style and the language should be free from verbose and clichés.
4. You should neither give personal experience, opinions nor use personal pronouns or direct speech except in quotations.
5. *Sentences*: The sentences should not be too involved or long and unwieldy.
6. You should avoid generalised or sweeping statements which are unsubstantiated.
7. *Organisation*: The thesis should be a well-organised whole developed in a sequence and in a linear fashion.
8. *Quotations*: Use quotations contextually and quote exactly with acknowledgements. You should acknowledge a quotation giving the reference particulars, in the footnotes/end notes, as per the norms given in *MLA handbook*. They should fit into the main running text by agreeing with subject and verb. If they do not fit in, omit certain words putting small dashes or dots.
9. If you don't acknowledge a quotation you will be charged with *plagiarism*[*], which is a serious academic crime or a sort of piracy.
10. *Signposting*: Assist your reader by signposting your argument by using appropriate linking words.
11. *Avoid*—
    a. First and second person pronouns; repetitions, excessive wordiness, too many quotations, overused phrases and clichés.
    b. Gender biased pronouns/terms and follow the guidelines of *MLA Handbook*.
    c. Spelling and Grammatical mistakes: No body will excuse the writer's spelling or grammatical mistakes and there is a limit for typographical mistakes.

---

[*] Refer to the Glossary

d. And follow consistently either British or American spelling. The computer spell check is helpful to some extent only and it is programmed to American spelling and usage. Better check the spell check done by the computer.
12. *Style*: Evolve your own style which should look like a natural flow but not imposed from above. "A good style should show no sign of effort. What is written should seem a happy accident"*

Format

Cover Page (Printed): It includes the *title* of the thesis and *scholar's name* which are printed and pasted on the hard cover of the book. The *degree* to which submitted (place), *university name, year* when submitted are also on the cover page.

Inner cover page: It is a replication of the cover page.

Declaration/Certificate♦ —A declaration statement by the research supervisor and declaration by the scholar will be included in the first few pages of the thesis.

i. Preface, ii. Acknowledgements, iii. Abstract, iv. Contents
1. Introduction, 2. Main body of the text – divided into chapters, 3. Conclusions.
Primary Sources, Secondary Sources, Bibliography or Selected Bibliography. Tables /Charts etc., if any.

Note:

There may be slight variations in the format from one university to another. Similarly, the number of copies to be submitted also differs.

♦ Somerset Maugham
♦ Variously called 'Signature Page'

4.4.6 Documenting Sources

The research and documentation online describes four commonly used systems of documentation. Documentation styles differ according to discipline. Scholars of humanities and arts use one kind and scholars of sciences use other kinds of style sheets (Guides). One among them is MLA style which is widely used by scholars of English and humanities.

For psychology and social sciences, the scholars use APA Style recommended by the American Psychological Association. It follows author and date system. Though the way of documenting sources in scientific publications are similar in many ways, the details of presenting source information vary from discipline to discipline and journal to journal. Major branches of sciences have their own names for their styles namely — *IEEE Standard Style Manual* for engineering (electrical and electronics), *Scientific Style and Format* for biological sciences, recommended by CBE (Council of Biology Editors) and *AMA Style Guide* for business writing.

But this chapter deals with the MLA style to give examples for writing bibliography cards and other purposes. If you are doing research in English or any other discipline in humanities, you use the norms set by the MLA style.

For more details you can refer to <www.dianahacker.com> or <www.bedfordstmartins.com>

4.4.6.1 *Preparing Bibliography Cards*

The information you copied on the bibliography cards is very useful not only as a data throughout your study but also to convert them as *Selected Bibliography, Works cited* list or *Selected List of Works Consulted* which you provide at the end of your thesis. You have to arrange them in the alphabetical order and put it at the end of the thesis. It means that the works cited are not confined to those referred to in the thesis but others also. The list of works cited at the end of the thesis will be helpful to the future scholars also who work on a similar topic/field.

How to Prepare Cards?

A Book with a single author

Generally, the cards made of cardboard with a size of 3" x 5" are used, for this purpose, so that they can be arranged in alphabetical order and lasts for a long time when you prepare the selected bibliography list at the end of your study.

Each card includes—— author's name, title of the book and publication information. You find these details on the inner cover page.

Example:

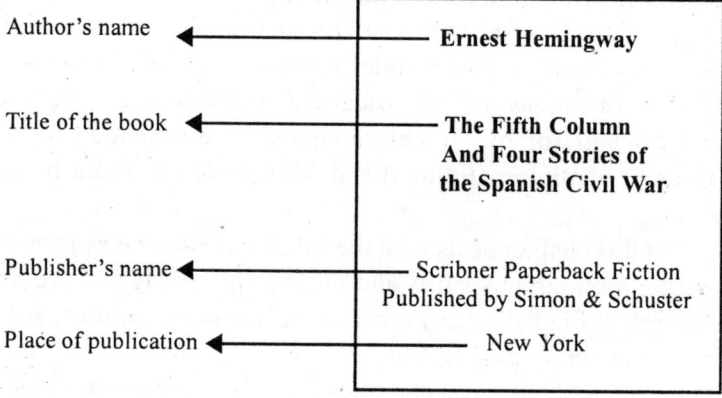

Author's name: When you prepare the bibliography card reverse the author's name i.e., Ernest Hemingway becomes——
Hemingway, Ernest. Use a comma after the first name, (Ernest) and a period (full stop) after completing the name.

Title of the book—copy the full title along with the subtitle, if there is one, put a colon after the main title underline the title and subtitle completely and put a period after the title. But do not underline the period.

Place of publication: New York. After you write the city where the book is published put colon.

Name of the Publisher: Give the name of the publisher and year of publication i.e,— Simon & Schuster, 1969. The year of publication will be given on a different page, inside the book, with a copyright symbol, (@).

Example 1:

If it is a book written by a single author, see the model below.

Your card now looks like this—

> Hemingway, Ernest.
>   *The Fifth Column:*
>   *And Four Stories of The Spanish Civil War.*
> New York: Simon & Schuster, 1969.

4.4.6.2 *A book with more than three authors*

Example:

If a book contains two authors, you reverse only the name of the first author, add a comma and give the other name of the authors in the normal order and place a period after the last name. And if the book contains more than three authors you name only the first one and add **'et al.'** after the first name of the author.

> Coe Norman, et al.
>   *Writing Skills: A Problem–solving Approach.*
>   Cambridge: Cambridge UP, 1983.

If it is a translation you write the abbreviation, 'trans' before the title.

If it has an editor you write abbreviation, 'ed' before title and rest of the things remain same.

4.4.6. 3 An Article from a Scholarly Journal

What do you do for citing a reference from a journal?
See the cover page for particulars:

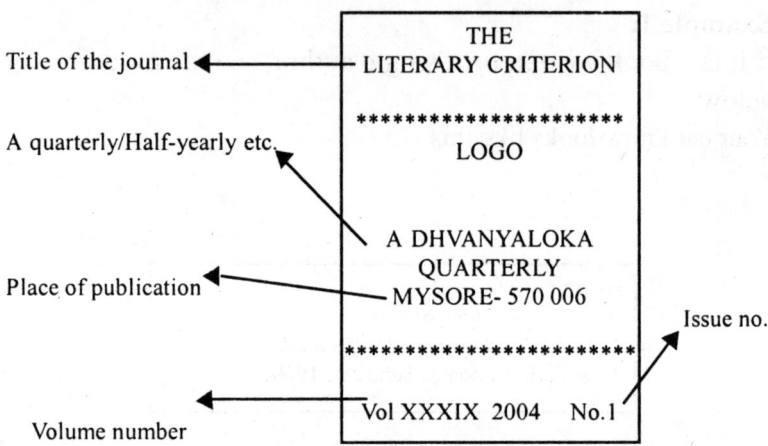

The cover page gives you —— 1. Title of the Journal — Literary Criterion: Quarterly
2. Place of Publication — Mysore; 3. Volume number — XXXIX;
5. Issue number — No. 1

About the Article ——For the details of article and name of the author see the inside of the journal.

Example:
Imagine you have to cite the following reference of an article from the above journal—
" Sankara's *Vivekachudamani:* A Philosophical text par excellence, S. Ramaswamy" Page No: 31-37

What do you do?
1. Reverse the name of the author 2. Write the title of the article in *double quotations* and 3. Write the full title of the journal and underline it. 4. The number of the volume should be followed by comma and 5 The year of the publication in brackets, followed by colon. 6. Lastly, the page numbers of the entire article should be noted and not the particular page which you used.

It will be as follows:
   Ramaswamy, S. "Sankara's Vivekachudamani: A Philosophical Text par excellence"
   The Literary Criterion 39 No 1 (2004): 31-37.

Note:
In the same way, you have to follow different rules when you cite an article from a newspaper, an article from a magazine or a review, and follow the norms set up by *MLA Handbook* or any other style depending upon the discipline you choose. You have to refer to the handbook to know the length of the margin and how much space should be left from the top, single or double line and other details.

4.4.6.4 *Documenting information from a website:*
The information, you copied or referred to from electronic sources like online periodical or website, should give sufficient information to allow the reader to locate it. Each kind of information needs different kind and amount of information to fulfil these objectives. The information, you give about the electronic media, which you cite, lacks an agreed format. Besides, the information one gives about, the electronic source is not as fixed as its print counterpart. You are expected to give minimum basic information about the electronic source. You should give at least three pieces of information–
1. Title of the site (underlined)
2. Editor's name (if given)
3. Electronic publication information, including version number, if available, latest update and name of any sponsoring institution or organisation
4. Date of access and URL If you are not able to give all the information as above, give whatever is available.

Examples:
An article from a journal online:
1. An article from online periodical:
Fowler, Alastair. "Shakespeare Fantasies" *The Times Literary Supplement*: A Literary Weekly
02 Feb 2005. http://www.the-tls.co.uk/this_week story. aspx? story id=2109861.
[Editor's name not available]

2. Website
Proofreading Symbols
Wordpeddler. Ed. Julies Shuffman. 5 January 2005. <http:/wordpeddler.com/symbols.htm>

Notes/ Footnotes/Endnotes:
When you document any source, it can appear either at the end of the text or at the bottom of the page. If it is written at the end of the text it is called *endnotes* and when it is written at the bottom of the relevant page it is *footnotes*. You may opt for either of them according to your suitability.

In the case of a research paper, the scholar has no choice except for using endnotes, unless they are instructed otherwise. But for thesis writing, the scholar may opt for footnotes or endnotes. Some use— notes and references, at the end of the chapter. You consult your supervisor. Both have certain advantages and disadvantages. The main advantage of endnotes is that you may write your remarks or any additional information.

Foot notes, as the name implies appear at the bottom of the page. You begin it four lines below the text. And keep single space between its lines.

Endnotes appear after the text or at the end of the chapter with the title, 'Notes' written at the centre of a fresh page with one inch from the top. And keep double space between the lines.

Unlike in the bibliography note, you don't reverse the author's name but write in the normal order followed by a comma. The notes includes—

1. Author's name (normal order)
2. The title
3. The publication data in parentheses and
4. Page reference. There is a full stop at the end. You use continuous number throughout the text.
5. Format note numbers as superscript (i.e., raised slightly above the line), without periods, parentheses or slashes. There is period only at the end.

Differences:

You might have noticed the main difference between a bibliography card and the footnotes or endnotes in terms of noting down the author's name etc. Another main difference is that there is no need of mentioning the page number(s) in the case of a bibliography card but you make a mention of the page numbers in the case of footnotes or endnotes.

Note: Follow *MLA Handbook* regulations strictly for standard abbreviations for popular publication details like Cambridge UP for Cambridge University Press, or GPO for Government Printing Press etc.

Proofreading Symbols:

It is better for the students of higher studies and scholars to be acquainted with the most common symbols* used in proofreading. Your supervisor may use these symbols while going through your draft thesis and you should be in a position to understand them and do corrections accordingly. There may be some variations from one kind and another. The symbols used by the journalists are slightly different from the following. Find some of them here——

Symbol	Meaning	Example
ℓ	Delete	The skills of advanced writing are never attained unless one is involved in it personally.
⁁	Insert a comma	*However* he failed to complete it.
⌄ ⌄	Double quotations	My favourite book is ⌄*Wings of Fire.*⌄
·	Use a period	One need not go from one library to another.
∧	Insert something	Ask him ∧to come here.
¶	Add a paragraph	
No ¶	No paragraph	
⌐	Transpose elements	She is only the one who got Ph. D
⌒	Close up	You can search some of the web sites.

* Taken from WordPeddler date: Jan 19. 2004 <http://wordpedddler.com/symbols.htm>

Some of the abbreviations often used:

Besides the above symbols used for proofreading you often find some abbreviations used by the research supervisor who goes through the thesis/dissertations. It is better if you are acquainted with the following—

\# — Number error (Singular plural)
ww— wrong word
poss —use possessive form
vt — verb tense error
S V agr —— subject —verb agreement
Pro agr —— pronoun agreement error —
rep — repetition
C, C – capitalisation error
P, —— punctuation error

Glossary

Bibliography : Bibliography is a list of readings about a particular subject.

Primary Sources: Primary sources include statistical data, historical documents on the topic chosen. They are the materials directly connected to the research topic.

Secondary Sources: Books, articles, political issues, historical events, or any writings about the topic or writer which are not directly related to them.

Plagiarism: Any passage of three or more words together borrowed without acknowledgement constitutes *plagiarism*.

Thesis Statement: It is simply a statement of your topic or problem which you are going to study and how you are going to deal with it.

Idea Sheets: They are big size cards (6+8) wherein you write all ideas kept in your mind connected with your topic. Or you may write questions, critical remarks, comments or anything which you hit upon regarding the topic.

Bibliography

Baugh, Sue L. *How to Write Term Papers and Reports,* Chicago: NTC Contemporary Publication group, 1997.

Bedekar, V. H. *How to Write Assignments, Research Papers, Dissertations and Thesis.* New Delhi: Kanak Publications, 1982

Berger, Asa Arthur. *Improving Writing Skills,* New Delhi: Sage Publications, 1993.

Bryant, Katherine, Newhouse Howard et. al, *Basic English: For Business Communication,* (Revised Edition) California: Pitman Learnic, 1984

Bryant, Miles T. *The Portable Dissertation Advisor,* California: Corwin Press, 2004.

Carrier, Michael. *Intermediate Language Skills: Writing,* London: Hodder and Stoughton, 1981

Coffin, Caroline and Mare Jane Curry et.al, *Teaching Academic Writing: A Toolbit for Higher Education,* London & NY Routledge, 2003.

Gibaldi, Joseph and S. Walter Achtert, *MLA Handbook for Writers of Research Papers,* (Sixth Edition), New Delhi: Affiliated East-West Press Pvt. Ltd. 2004.

Ingram Beverly & King Carol, *From Writing to Composing: An Introductory Composition Course for Students of English,* Cambridge: CUP, 1988.

Jones, Leo. *Progress to Proficiency,* Great Britain: OUP, 1986.

Jones, Leo. *Functions of English,* 1977; Oxford, OUP, 1990

Jordan, R.R. *Academic Writing Course,* (Collins Study Skills), 1980; London: Addison Wesley, 1997

Kaplan, Robert B. and A. Peter Shaw, *Exploring Academic Discourse,* London: Newbury House Publishing Inc, 1983.

Kingsbury, Roy & Wellman Guy, *Read and Write,* Great Britain: Longman Group Ltd, 1988.

Mounsey, Chris, *Essays and Dissertations,* Oxford: OUP, 2002

Philips, Estelle M. & D. S, Paugh. *How to Get a Ph D,* Milton Keynes: Philadelphia, Open Univ Press, 1987.

*****